T0118432

100 Questions Answered

PRESIDENT DONALD TRUMP'S SIGNATURE

Analysis and Synthesis

ILYAS M. ZESHAN

Archway Publishing books may be ordered through booksellers or by contacting:

Archway Publishing
1663 Liberty Drive
Bloomington, IN 47403
www.archwaypublishing.com
1 (888) 242-5904

ISBN: 978-1-4808-7077-2 (sc)
ISBN: 978-1-4808-7076-5 (hc)
ISBN: 978-1-4808-7078-9 (e)

Library of Congress Control Number: 2018965996

Print information available on the last page.

Archway Publishing rev. date: 01/17/2019

Dedicated to

My Friend Lori
and
My Students
and
My Clients

Contents

Questions Asked about the Legitimacy of Handwriting Analysis

Questions asked from 2017-2018

Foreign Relations

Questions asked from 2015-2016

Pictorial Dictionary

My Take

Nearly twenty years ago, I was analyzing a great number of celebrity handwritings and signatures. During that period I came across President Trump's signature. I analyzed his signature and answered a few questions and then moved to the next celebrity.

Since President Trump announced his candidacy for president, I have received a barrage of questions. Whenever I go to small meetings, large meetings, or one-on-one meetings, people's questions just keep pouring. Some questions were asked over and over by different folks in different styles. At that point I began taking mental note of those questions and jotting them down after the meetings. What you see here is a collection of questions asked prior to and after Mr. Trump assumed the office of the presidency. These questions were paraphrased and shortened in some cases. Similar questions were combined if they were asked by more than one person. These questions were answered in the light of established principles of Handwriting Analysis. You will find generic analysis followed by synthesis that contains explanations and elaboration. Hundreds of questions were asked, but I selected 100 questions.

The only criteria were that they must be of good taste, nonpartisan, and asked on more than one occasion.

The questions posed in shaded language were excluded. Also, I divided questions into two parts in a descending order. The first part includes questions asked from 2017 to 2018. The second part addresses questions asked from 2015 to 2016.

I decided not to include the technical aspects of how I arrived at the conclusions in answering every question. Instead I have included a pictorial dictionary of strokes at the end of the book. I give technical explanations when I teach this subject. In my experience, I discovered the average person is only interested in the end result rather than the complex, boring and technical explanations.

The purpose of writing the book is to quench the thirst of inquiring minds and for entertainment purposes only. Every care has been taken so that no word or phrase will be misconstrued as offensive or disrespectful to the president or anyone else.I would appreciate your comments on the series of questions covered in this book.

Please email your feedback to
ILYASZESHAN@gmail.com

"Spoken words are the symbol of mental experience and written words are the symbols of the spoken words."

Aristotle

---

3 Personalities

All of us have three personalities,

(1) what we think we are,
(2) what others think we are,
(3) what we really are.

All three personalities have discrepancies. Handwriting Analysis deals with number three – what we really are!

I learned a great deal about National and International politics by using Handwriting Analysis as a tool

Handwriting is a portrait of the writer's brain

President's Signature

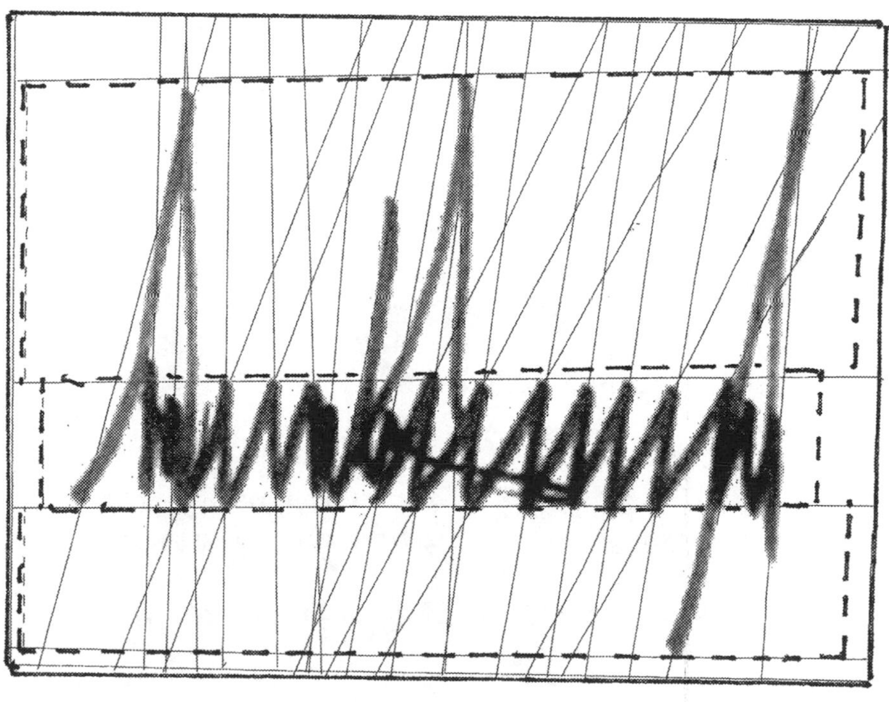

Graphological Features of President's Signature

The following technical graphological features are exclusively for the people who studied and practiced graphology.

Macro Graphological Features

1. Signature size 150% to 200% larger than rest of the handwriting
2. All three zones are exaggerated
3. Upper zone is dominant out of all three zones
4. Lower zone is uneven
5. Middle zone varies, some letters are dwarfed
6. Pen pressure excessively high
7. Legibility is average
8. Absence of garland and arcade formation in the middle zone letters
9. Curves are virtually non-existent
10. Angle of letter range from 55-95 degrees including handwriting

Micro Graphological Features

1. Capital 'D' starts with initial stroke
2. Height of 'D' is five times the width of letters

3. Top of the 'D' sharply pointed
4. Top of the 'D' twisted
5. Capital 'D' angle 75 degrees in most of signatures
6. Downward stroke in capital 'D' is near 90 degrees
7. 'D's' upward slant slightly curved
8. 'D's' downward stroke with no curve
9. Second letter 'o' is concealed in Capital 'D'
10. 'o' is dwarfed compared to other middle zone letters
11. 'o' is partly filled with ink
12. 'o' is looped double
13. Tiny double loop in 'o' is invisible
14. Small 'n' is uncurved
15. Angle of letter 'n' is 75 to 85 degrees in most signatures
16. Small letter 'a' is compressed
17. Small letter 'a' is double looped
18. Small letter *'l'*is retraced
19. Small letter *'l'* is four times taller than other middle zone letters in most signatures
20. Small letter 'd' is dwarfed
21. Small letter 'd' is partly filled with ink
22. Capital 'T' is 5 times taller than middle zone letters
23. Angle of 'T' is parallel to capital 'D'

24. Capital 'T' is twisted at the top
25. Top of Capital 'T' is conical
26. Small letter 'r' blended with other middle zone letters
27. Small 'u' is excessively angular
28. Small letter 'm' is with no curves
29. Small letter 'p' is embellished
30. Small letter 'p' is even taller than the rest of the capitals in most signatures
31. Letter 'p' with a twist at the top occasionally
32. P's upper zone is dominant
33. P's slant more than 90 degree angle

Questions Asked about The Legitmacy of Handwriting Analysis

Signature Analysis

Question 1

I have been hearing your explanations about the president's signature. I have never heard about Signature Analysis or Handwriting Analysis before. Could you please briefly explain what signature analysis is all about?

Answer 1

Handwriting Analysis is a valuable and short method of discovering and evaluating a writer's inner personality by examining the peculiarities of his or her handwriting. Handwriting Analysis is based on definite laws. It is backed by statistical data and meaningful research. This is the evolution of the study of doodles, drawings, and paintings.

The assessment of handwriting is similar to assessing a person's emotional and mental state of mind through facial expressions, handshakes, the tone of his or her voice, and his or her body gestures.

Handwriting originates not from the hand as commonly believed but from the brain, and it is stimulated by brain impulses. Handwriting is a portrait of the writer's brain.

Handwriting Reveals a Person's Character

Question 2

My question is not about the president's signature, but I want to know why handwriting reveals a person's character.

Answer 2

Any physical movement, whether body movements, gestures, facial expressions, voices, or sounds, all characterize the human personality.

Handwriting is a peculiar physical movement that requires concentration along with the five motor skills and the influence of emotions.

Handwriting is pretty similar to body language. No matter how you were taught at an early age, your handwriting will develop a style according to your values and feelings that will uniquely reflect your true personality as you grow older.

Scope of Handwriting Analysis

Question 3

I am quite astonished by the way you described the president's signature. I am wondering what the scope of Signature Analysis is. There must be some part of the personality that handwriting cannot reveal. Also, can people disguise their handwriting?

Answer 3

Handwriting Analysis can reveal what state of mind the writer was in at the time he or she put the pen to the paper. It tells us about their hidden talents and skills. It reveals aspects of their personality that are not consistent with their appearance.

An in-depth analysis will uncover the disguised meaning of the words than that of handwritings. Disguising is nearly impossible in an adequate sample of handwriting.

Handwriting also sheds light on a person's past and present, cultivations and growth, and how their life has developed through different stages of time.

Handwriting matures as the person --grows. It also shows a sign of aging and disintegration as well as mental, emotional, and physical ailments.

Trust in Handwriting Analysis

Question 4

My question is very simple. I am curious to know how much Signature Analysis be trusted. How reliable and scientific is this subject?

Answer 4

The best way to discover the reliability of Handwriting Analysis is to start to analyze your own handwriting. That will be the quickest way to prove to yourself that you are the one who knows yourself best.

I am pretty sure that once you finish reading the book, you will be self-conscious about your own handwriting as you begin to see your strengths and weaknesses vividly.

Handwriting Analysis is conducted in the same scientific fashion as fingerprint analysis.

Painstaking research has proven over and over that the pen strokes and formation of letters zero in on the human personality.

My Handwriting Changes

Question 5

I am a little surprised about the science of Handwriting Analysis. Why can Handwriting Analysis interpretations be trusted when my handwriting changes all the time?

Answer 5

Handwriting changes in accordance with a person's mood and thinking process. Some changes are short-term while others last longer. Short-term changes can be observed as a result of people's quick tempers, their temporary illnesses, or if they are under the influence of alcohol. Once these people have calmed down, recuperated, or recovered from a hangover, their handwriting will return to normal.

A regression in handwriting will show if there is a chronic disease, a sudden loss of wealth, a devastating death in the family, or a nasty divorce. All will show regression in handwriting.

On the positive side, a sudden windfall of wealth, meeting the person of your dreams, or an improvement in health will produce progressive handwriting.

The bottom line is that changes in handwriting reflect the impact of the circumstances of an individual's life whether they are positive or negative.

Looks of the Handwriting

Question 6

I consider myself a good person. I am a law-abiding citizen. My handwriting is sloppy. How can you justify this?

Answer 6

Pen strokes and the formation of letters matter most when it comes to incorporating handwriting, not the look of the handwriting per se.

A beautiful calligrapher is not necessarily a good or positive person. Calligraphy is a form of drawing, not writing, and is done with conscious efforts to follow the strict rules of calligraphy. On the other hand, doctors have a reputation of having sloppy handwriting. Sloppiness in handwriting does not make them a bad person. What matters in Handwriting Analysis are the strokes not the look of the writing.

History of Handwriting Analysis

Question 7

I am quite fascinated by the way you described the president's signature. What is the background or history of Signature Analysis? How long has this been around?

Answer 7

Ancient handwriting has been the subject of intense interest amongst many observers. Aristotle said, "Spoken words are the symbol of mental experience and written words are the symbols of spoken words."

In the seventeenth century, Dr. Camillo Baldin of the University of Bologna wrote a book that led to the spread of interest in Handwriting Analysis throughout Europe, especially in Germany, France, and Switzerland.

A great number of scholarly books have been published on this subject throughout Europe and the United States in the last couple of centuries.

Foot Writing and Mouth Writing

Question 8

I have heard quite a bit about Handwriting Analysis. I have a hard time believing that handwriting can tell so much. Can you give a little synopsis of how it works?

Answer 8

Handwriting is closely connected with the brain. First, the image develops in the brain and then transmits the information through the nervous system to the arms and hands to make handwriting possible.

There have been numerous experiments conducted on people writing with their feet or holding pens in their mouths. The formation of their letters fundamentally stays the same. Since it is dictated by the brain, it is called "brain writing," and handwriting is a pseudo name.

Legitimacy of Handwriting Analysis

Question 9

I have a question about the legitimacy of handwriting analysis. If it is a scientific subject some professionals must be using it, correct?

Answer 9

A great number of psychologists use Handwriting Analysis as a secondary tool for studying their clients' behaviors. They seek Handwriting Analysts' help in this regard. During the patients' treatment, a psychologist monitors their clients' handwriting to look for signs of improvement.

One part of Handwriting Analysis is known as "questioned document examination," where lawyers and law enforcement authorities verify the authenticity of the subject's handwriting. Handwriting experts compare the forged handwriting with the original document and put forward their opinions.

Personnel departments often use the services of Handwriting Analysts to determine the abilities in order to recruit the most qualified person out of all the applicants.

Clergies and social workers use Handwriting Analysis quite often to comprehend the habits and addictions of their clients.

Marriage counselors use handwriting to find the most common denominators and compatibility factors between two individuals to make the relationship more successful.

Deliberately Changing Handwriting

Question 10

Like other gentlemen, I am skeptical about Handwriting Analysis. If a person purposely changed his or her handwriting, won't that misinterpretation also be changed?

Answer 10

In case the writer deliberately alters his or her handwriting in order to misguide the Handwriting Analysts, he or she may succeed in an area of lesser significance in a smaller sample of writing. But the analyst can easily catch the person when they consult a previously written sample of handwriting and compare that with the sample of handwriting in question.

Handwriting Therapy
Graphotherapy

Question 11

I heard somewhere that there is such a thing called handwriting therapy. Is that true?

Answer 11

Since Handwriting Analysis is a scientific subject, it works both ways. If you change your handwriting, your personality will change, and if you change your habits, then your handwriting will change, without a conscious effort. As we change, our handwriting changes automatically.

You can strengthen your virtues and remedy your vulnerabilities. It is a great tool. The theory of handwriting therapy is that your thinking process affects your handwriting. In reverse, your handwriting will influence your thinking process. Handwriting therapy can help you to enrich your life.

Questions asked from 2017 to 2018

Please email your feedback to
ILYASZESHAN@gmail.com

Salesman-in-Chief

Question 12

I am very curious to know about what made the president so successful in the private sector and now in public life. He must have some secret formula. Have you tried to figure out his secret method from his signature?

□ Analysis

- A desire to perform so great that he can turn his dreams into a reality
- Ability to motivate people with the power of pleasure and pain
- Ability to turn a disappointing situation into an opportunity

O Synthesis

The president's skills and talents are unlimited, which is manifested in his signature. He has polished and perfected his sales skills beyond the comprehension of an average person. Without a doubt, his ability to sell is his best skill. Every action he takes, every word he utters translates into proven sales principles. He applies and executes all sales methods in every step of the way. In every sales concept, he sees a "thousand points of light."

These sales skills made him successful in a private sector. He is applying the same principles in public life. With his vast knowledge and experience, it would not be inappropriate to call him salesman-in-chief.

Leading Cause of Stress—Reality

Question 13

I was reading in the newspaper that the president sleeps few hours, tweets at 3:00 a.m., and works long hours. He must be stressed out quite a bit. Does his signature show signs of stress?

☐ Analysis

- High level of endurance
- Enjoys what he does
- Expects from people more than their capabilities

O Synthesis

The president's signature indicates that he possesses powerful stamina. His signature doesn't show any sign of serious fatigue. He does only what he enjoys and delegates the rest to others. He would probably be more stressed out if he didn't do anything.

As far as the 3:00 a.m. tweets are concerned, he likes to send the message that he is alert and in control at anytime of the day or night. He runs a tight ship. Sometimes he expects people to bite more than they can chew. He has an uncontrollable urge to perform.

When he sees his program is not progressing in accordance to his expectation, he may become stressed. The leading cause of stress is reality.

Tweets Galore

Question 14

The president's constant tweets have become the subject of great interest. People are getting curious about why he chooses to comment through tweets so often. Can any conclusion be drawn from his signature?

☐ Analysis

- Use of sales principles always in his mind
- Prefers to communicate directly
- Hates lengthy explanations

○ Synthesis

Handwriting Analysis or Signature Analysis cannot reveal whether a writer tweets or not. However, examining a writer's use or recurring actions may provide a clue for that tendency.

From the president's signature, it is quite obvious that sales and the techniques that make sales possible are always on his mind. He makes a sales pitch whenever and wherever he gets a chance. Tweets carry certain characteristics that correspond to the president's style of pitch.

One of the pillars of his communication is that his messages must be direct and precise. In sales, this method is known as KISS, which stands for "keep it simple and short." Tweets perfectly fit in that scenario, and the president loves it.

Dissatisfaction Gives Him Satisfaction

Question 15

I wonder what makes the president happy and content. Does it show in his signature?

☐ **Analysis**

- Wish list unlimited
- Hard to please
- Never content
- Gigantic projects turn him on

○ **Synthesis**

From the president's standpoint, happiness and contentment are two different notions. This is indicated in his signature. When he attains his goal, he feels happy for the time being, but he's not satisfied. Dissatisfaction gives him satisfaction.

He is always moving his goalpost forward. To him, satisfaction means he accomplished all, which is never acceptable to him. He feels good when things are kicking and moving forward continuously.

Unpredictability

Question 16

The president takes pride in saying, "I want to remain unpredictable!" I am wondering how unpredictable the president is. What does his signature point to?

☐ **Analysis**

- Loves surprises
- Enjoys leaving subject matter as a cliff-hanger
- Adores seeing people in a state of bewilderment

○ **Synthesis**

Handwriting experts agree that an extrovert and passionate person is more predictable than a meek, introverted individual. The president's signature categorically describes that he is an ocean of emotions.

Strong, extraverted people have more constants than variables in their handwriting as far as traits are concerned. This makes them more predictable unless they, with exception, make a conscious effort to prove the other wrong. In that case, he picks up the option against his wishes.

Another scenario is that writers alter his handwriting to mislead the handwriting analyst. In that case, multiple samples that are written at different periods of time are needed. The president holds values that are deep-seated. It will be pretty hard for him to violate them.

Glass Half Full?

Question 17

The President sounds optimistic all the time. Does he see the glass half full or half empty according to his signature?

☐ **Analysis**

- Extremely hopeful
- A feeling that he can surmount any challenge
- Keeps morale high at all times

○ **Synthesis**

The president's signature clearly tells that he feels optimistic at all times. He feels that he carries so many arrows in his belt that he can knock down any challenge, at any time, coming from any direction. He is extremely confident in his communication skills. He never allows negative thoughts to enter his mind. He keeps his morale high at all times.

Sometimes he sees things in a unique way. Certainly, he sees the glass as half full. Once in a while, he feels that the glass was built twice the size it is supposed to be.

President Trump and Mrs. Clinton

Sales Ability v. Technocratic Ability

Question 18

What was the dominant reason that the president succeeded in the last election and Mrs. Clinton couldn't make it? Does his signature provide any explanation?

☐ Analysis

- Sales ability v. technocratic ability

○ Synthesis

President Trump and Mrs. Clinton's signatures indicate that both possess a different set of skills. The president's skills are geared toward sales, and Mrs. Clinton is well versed in technocratic abilities. The president carries a natural sales ability while Mrs. Clinton is a natural technocrat. Generally, technocrats always wonder and are sometimes envious why salespeople make so much money and receive recognition, while technocrats spend so much time in learning and schooling. The past election was a contest between a salesperson and a technocrat. Salespeople make things happen, and technocrats wonder what happened.

More Focus on the Other Side of the Fence

Question 19

The president's victory in the election stunned the nation. Does his signature show any key strategy elements that made this success possible?

☐ **Analysis**

- Focusing more on opponents' weaknesses more than his own strengths
- A belief in personalized approach rather than a cookie-cutter one
- Ability to embellish and inflate opponents' weaknesses

○ **Synthesis**

In any competitive situation, the president focuses more on the challenger's weak areas where he can hit hard rather than capitalizing on his own strengths. As he inflates his opponents' vulnerabilities, their shortcomings make them look much worse than they really are.

He is always curious to know what is happening on the other side of the fence and makes himself ready to surprise his opponents with a counterpunch.

1

Transactional Friendship

Question 20

I have a short question. I just want to know how friendly the president is. What do you see in his signature?

☐ Analysis

- Believes in transactional friendships

O Synthesis

The short answer is yes. He is friendly, but his signature tells that he doesn't believe in conventional friendships. He is always wearing sales glasses. He sees even friendships from a sales viewpoint. There is an acronym in sales known as WIIFM. *What is in it for me?* If he finds a convincing answer, he will be a great friend.

Hates Partnership

Question 21

The president is a great businessman and entrepreneur. However, there must be some part of the business that he doesn't' like. Can you name any aspect of the business from his signature that he is not comfortable with?

☐ **Analysis**

- No tolerance for equal partner
- Hates details in general

○ **Synthesis**

The president's signature reveals that there are some parts of the business that he loves more than others. What he loves most is the sales aspect of the business, and what he likes least are details and research.

He is certainly uncomfortable with having an equal partner in business. He will tolerate a partner who plays the role of a sleeping partner.

Acting Presidential

Question 22

The President has been in office for more than one hundred days, yet he is criticized for not acting presidential. What is stopping him from doing that? Does his signature give any clue?

☐ Analysis

- Deep-rooted habits
- Hates changes of any sort
- More comfortable in casual environment

O Synthesis

The word *change* is one of the few words that the president hates most. This is highlighted in his signature. He prefers to move the table rather than moving his chair. He doesn't like changing himself. He feels that he is in the business to bring changes in others. He expects and sometimes demands that people must accept him the way he is. He also believes people will get used to him eventually. Acting presidential causes him discomfort. In his view he should be free to act as he pleases rather than acting to please others.

Addiction

Question 23

My question is about addiction. So far we know that the president doesn't have any conventional addictions like smoking or drinking. Does his signature show some other kinds of addiction that we are not aware of?

☐ Analysis

- Being a workaholic
- Joy in taking risk
- An urge to invite challenges

○ Synthesis

The president's addictions are unconventional and intangible. He likes to remain busy at all times. He is not an alcoholic but he is certainly a workaholic. The more he works hard, the more he gets high. He not only works hard, but he also plays hard. It seems that it is his high energy that pushes him to work hard. In reality and without realizing it, he works hard to get rid of the extra energy that pesters him.

A Craving to Direct the Wind Rather than Adjust the Sail

Question 24

A friend of mine is a psychologist. He was telling me that the president's ability to adapt is on the low side. I am just curious to know whether that shows in his signature?

☐ Analysis

- Severe inflexibility
- Values are engraved in stone
- Extreme desire to control
- Pragmatic thinking

O Synthesis

The President's signature vividly points out that adaptability and flexibility is not his cup of tea. He craves to adjust the wind rather than adjusting the sail. He hates to follow rules set by someone else. His signature also indicates that his inner desire must be to run as an independent. He feels uncomfortable working within the parameters of the Republican Party. Practicality compelled him to swallow the pill and embrace the Republican Party.

Any Commonality with President Nixon?

Question 25

I am hearing quite a bit that President Trump has much in common with President Nixon. Have you found similarities between the two presidents?

☐ Analysis

- Very little in common between the two presidents
- President Trump is an extrovert. President Nixon was an introvert.

O Synthesis

I couldn't discover much commonality between the two presidents except that both are driven to make their name in history.

President Nixon wanted to set records that no future president would be able to break. President Trump wants to break all previous presidents' records. The fact that President Nixon was an introvert and President Trump is an extrovert is indicated in their signatures.

President Nixon was interested in knowing more about what was happening outside the borders of the United States, while President Trump is more interested in knowing what is happening within the United States. Meeting with foreigners was a turn-on for President Nixon. However, meeting with foreigners is a turn-off for President Trump unless he sees something that he can learn from their experiences.

Sentimentalism and Rationalism

Question 26

In the president's signature, what is the single most important trait or technique that allowed him to emerge successfully in the election while Mrs. Clinton could not?

☐ Analysis

- Ability to arouse people's emotions
- Ability to do or say something that captures the imagination of his audience

O Synthesis

The president's ability to arouse the emotions of people was the single most important technique used throughout his campaign. The entire strategy was focused on intensifying people's emotions. This is rather easy for him. The president is a passionate being, which is vividly obvious in his signature.

On the other hand, Mrs. Clinton's approach was to appeal to people's logic and intellect. Psychologists agree that when there is a struggle between the conscious mind, which represents logic, and the subconscious mind, which represents emotions, the subconscious mind always wins the struggle.

Sales people rarely make a pitch to a potential buyer in order to appeal to their logical mind. Their presentation is primarily focused on touching their emotions. This is especially true when they deal with those who are non-business people or average consumers.

Impeachment

Question 27

Quite a few people have been talking about the president's impeachment since day one. Now there is a commercial going on about his impeachment. Does the president's signature indicate that he will be impeached?

☐ Analysis

- High degree of resentment
- A belief can control anyone at anytime
- A feeling that people are generally naïve

O Synthesis

Handwriting analysis doesn't make future predictions. Its scope is limited to personality assessments. However, reaction can be assessed from an action. Talking about or promoting the idea of impeachment is a bad idea. The president feels he is unimpeachable because he is incapable of doing anything wrong. Promoters of impeachment should not be surprised when they see his 'fire and fury.' It would lead to nothing but a deepening of the divisions.

Election 2020

Question 28

Can you make any predictions about the next election? Will President Trump be in the White House in 2020?

Answer

Making predictions is beyond the scope of handwriting analysis. Handwriting analysis is only limited to personality assessment. However, some forecast can be made about how one will act or react in given circumstance.

I have been asked numerous times to make a forecast about the Super Bowl. So far I have an excellent record. In order to make a Super Bowl forecast, I require all team players' signatures. Then I do a comparative study.

If you pose this question after the nomination of both parties, I will be better equipped to make some sort of assessment by comparing the signatures of both nominees at that time.

Experience Is Superior to Learning

Question 29

The president has been in the office for more than six months. We are still hearing that a great number of positions have not been filled. The president is a great employer in the private sector. Why is it taking so long to fill the vacancies? Does his signature show what he looks for in a prospective employee?

□ Analysis

- Skills with common sense
- Practical experience is more important than college degrees

O Synthesis

The president is always looking for someone who is not only a proficient worker but also will be an asset in some shape or form to the organization. Skill combined with loyalty and common sense is very important to him. The president's signature indicates that practicality is a supreme priority. Experience without learning is better than learning without experience.

A Strong Belief that Business Opens Business

Question 30

We know that the president is a great businessman. Do you see something special in his signature that made him such a great entrepreneur?

☐ Analysis

- Abundant entrepreneurial spirit
- Ability to take optimum advantage of a situation
- Ability to recognize opportunities where most people do not

O Synthesis

Without a doubt, the president is an entrepreneur at heart. His signature indicates this fact. He possesses all the traits that are required to be an adroit entrepreneur. He is always wearing his entrepreneurial glasses.

He sees a business in everything like an artist sees beauty in everything or a humorist sees wit in every word. He believes business opens business.

No Criticism Is Too Small

Question 31

Why does the President get involved in petty point scoring? Why doesn't he just ignore certain comments and move forward? What does his signature say about this?

☐ Analysis

- No tolerance for any sort of criticism
- No criticism is too small
- Possesses a feeling of being flawless

○ Synthesis

The President's signature shows that he bears zero tolerance for criticism in any shape or form. His signature also indicates that he carries an overblown ego. He perceives himself to be flawless and likes to portray the image that he can do no wrong. He believes his critics misconstrue his image and spin his statements.

Gun Control, Import and Export of Values

Question 32

School shootings have become a frequent phenomenon. The president has put forward some suggestions on how to stop this madness. Can you tell from his signature how serious he is about wiping out these tragic occurrences?

☐ Analysis

- See value on both sides of the issue
- Any suggestions on reform turn him on
- Make decisions based on intended goal

O Synthesis

Gun control continues to be a subject of exhausting debate and some people are getting nauseated. More guns or less guns, where is the magic solution hidden? The simple answer is in neither scenario.

This is an intangible issue of a tangible problem. This is a question of values and indoctrination.

Seeing a solution in more guns is the evolution or the remnants of the 'wild wild west' culture. Pleading for less guns is an international ideas. Foreign countries experience less violence because they have fewer guns.

What is currently happening is that, the coastal United States is pleading for fewer guns because they are more in tune with international values.

The new phenomenon is that the millennial of the heartland are downloading international values on their computers and cell phones every day. This is a form of cyber attack on the heartland values. Millennial tend to agree with the views of coastal United States. Millennial are fatigued with their parent's old values and now their mission is to shake hands with coastal residents of the United States – the sooner the better.

Breaking Records

Question 33

What makes the President turn-on most? Is it wealth, fame, or something else?

☐ **Analysis**

- Loves to break records

○ **Synthesis**

Wealth and fame are certainly a turn-on for the president. His signature indicates that he feels wealth and fame are the means, not the end. The end is recognition. Somehow, he feels that breaking previous records set by his predecessors as the ultimate recognition. His biggest turn-on is leaving everybody behind.

Diplomatic Protocols

Question 34

A friend of mine was telling me that the president hates diplomatic protocols. Does this show in his signature? What could possibly the reason?

☐ Analysis

- High degree of rigidity
- Hates to follow instruction
- Any action out of habit is perceived as an unnatural act

○ Synthesis

This is an interesting observation. His signature shows that he is uncomfortable with some diplomatic protocols. He doesn't like anything that is mandatory. Diplomatic protocols fall into this category because he feels it is some sort of imposition.

Since the president has an inflexible personality, anything out of his normal habits are perceived by him as a forced act. However, he will swallow essential protocols. Deep down, he feels formality is a form of hypocrisy.

Judging the Judges

Question 35

Why is the president so uncomfortable with judges and the judiciary? Why does he criticize them? Does his signature indicate a reason for this discomfort?

☐ Analysis

- Judgmental outlook
- A feeling that no one can make a better decision than he can
- Arrive on conclusion based on previously held view

○ Synthesis

This is not a question of criticizing judges or the judiciary. Rather this is a reaction of feeling that no one can make a better decision than he can. He perceives his thinking to be superior to the judges. He feels that the interpretations of these judges are a reflection of thinking inside the box.

The president's signature also indicates that he carries a judgmental propensity. Judgmental people do not like to be judged. They feel this is their exclusive territory.

Another reason is the president's private sector background where there is no judicial interference. The CEO's word is always the last word.

Disparaging Own Party Leaders

Question 36

Ronald Reagan once said, "Never criticize a fellow republican." We see the president disparage senior senators and congressmen. Even leaders from within his own party are not spared. What kind of wisdom is that? Does his signature give a clued into this rationale?

☐ Analysis

- A belief that push and pull draws attention
- A belief that applying pressure create solution and results
- A belief that discouragement motivates people more than encouragement

O Synthesis

The president's signature indicates that he will use any conceivable tool to get the job done as efficiently as possible.

The president's unique approach rests in his belief that he can offend the cook, even if he expects a delicious dinner. The reason being is to persuade the cook not to let his guard down and prepare an even more delicious dinner. A temporary tease would result in greater efficiency and productivity and a permanent excitement.

He doesn't create this sort of connection consciously. It comes to him naturally.

More Monologue, Less Dialogue

Question 37

Unlike previous presidents, this administration doesn't conduct as many business briefings and press conferences. What conclusion can be drawn from the president's signature?

□ Analysis

- A belief that monologue is better than dialogue
- A belief that *worse to bad is good*
- A belief that less talk will result in more control

O Synthesis

The president's signature vividly indicates that he believes in monologue more than dialogue. His signature also indicates he believes that less feedback means less room for spreading rumors and that public relations can be managed better. No press conference will open the door to only one criticism. However, conducting frequent press conferences will open the door to numerous questions that will result in numerous criticisms.

Predominant Vocabulary—Sales Vocabulary

Question 38

The president has been criticized from different corners who say that he possesses a limited vocabulary. To my knowledge, he graduated from a prestigious university. Why doesn't he speak college-level English? Does his signature shed light on this phenomenon?

□ Analysis

- Takes extreme pride in his specialized skills
- More comfortable mingling with selected people
- Deep-seated likes and dislikes

○ Synthesis

This is a question of specialized knowledge rather than a limited vocabulary. The president's most specialized knowledge and skills are in sales. His dominant thoughts are always on what sells and what doesn't. On any occasion, he injects sales principles one way or the other. There are several kinds of vocabularies, such as casual, corporate, diplomatic, technical, and so on. The president uses sales phrases, jargon, and vocabulary. One of the cardinal rules in sales is to speak in the most common denominator.

Amendment Needs to be Amended

Question 39

The president seems frustrated with media criticism. Some newspapers continuously give him bad reviews. Why does he not lower his rhetoric? What does his signature say?

☐ Analysis

- A belief his job is to give orders and not the other way around
- Wants sweet without sour
- Inflexible views

O Synthesis

The president's signature says that he takes direction from no one. It is the other party's job to bow or make adjustments. He might not utter a word, but subliminally, he feels that the First Amendment is flawed and needs to be amended.

Rehashing the Story

Question 40

People point out that the president often repeats himself. Does this have something to do with his memory or something that we do not know? What does his signature suggest?

□ Analysis

- Closely follows sales principles
- Sharp memory
- A belief that people do not believe him

O Synthesis

The president's signature indicates that he possesses a sharp memory. Old memories are as fresh as those events that happened yesterday. There are two reasons why he repeats the story often. One, he has a feeling that people don't believe him. He wants to make people believe by repetition. Two, he follows established sales principles. The theory is that people have a short memory. Eighty percent of people forget 80 percent of the story 80 percent of the time.

Sales experts insist that the successful pitch must be based on three steps. First, tell them what you are going to tell. Second, tell your story, and third, tell them what you have just told.

The President and the Presidency

Question 41

We know that this president is very unconventional. Occasionally, he responds in such a manner that doesn't seem appropriate for a president. Why does he do that? Can you draw any conclusion from his signature?

☐ Analysis

- A feeling of being larger than life
- Feels that he deserves better praise after attaining his goals

O Synthesis

The president's signature vividly points out that he possesses an image of himself higher than people perceive him. People respect him because he is occupying the seat of the presidency. He feels that he should be respected regardless. He is larger than the presidency. He carries mixed feelings. He is proud that he left everybody behind, but he still has a long way to go.

Health, Wealth, and Wisdom

Question 42

I am curious to know what the president's signature indicates about what he takes pride in—that is, other than being the president.

☐ Analysis

- Extreme pride in his health
- Extreme pride in his wealth
- Extreme pride in his wisdom

O Synthesis

The president is proud of anything and everything he does. He might not talk about these things in public, but he will brag about even his dark secrets in his inner circle. Why brag about his dark secrets? Just to get a clap from his friends to prove that he can do something nobody can.

The president takes pride in his health. He feels that he is healthier than a sumo wrestler. Certainly, he takes pride in his wealth, especially the innovative techniques he used to make his financial success possible.

He takes pride in the feeling that his intelligence is unmatched. He feels that he can accept any challenge from anyone on any issue and exhaust his opponent to a point of nausea.

Different Strokes for Different Folks

Question 43

The president said that he is the least discriminatory person you could ever meet. Does the president's signature show that he treats everybody equally?

☐ Analysis

- A belief in different strokes for different folks
- A belief that the world is heterogeneous
- A belief that life is unfair

O Synthesis

The president's signature indicates that people have very different potentials. They should be treated in accordance with their potential. Everyone needs special consideration. There should be different strokes for different folks.

An Unwinding Tool—Rally

Question 44

Election season is over, and the president is still conducting rallies. Have you tried to figure out from his signature why he is conducting rallies?

☐ Analysis

- Sees rally as a feel-good endeavor
- Positive charged crowds make him doubly energized
- Gets furious if interrupted when he is making a point

○ Synthesis

The president's signature indicates that he enjoys lecturing more than speaking. Being a keynote speaker is a big turn-on for him. He is doubly pleased when people pay undivided attention to him. As a matter of fact, he demands that level of attention and a place where heckling is not permitted.

Since the president is in the habit of conducting sales seminars, he enjoys rallies because they fall in the same category.

Undivided attention, a flow of positive energy, sole occupation of the stage, and respect that is close to the level of worship is a mega turn-on for him.

After receiving and enduring criticism, he uses a rally as an unwinding tool. He also wants the whole world to know that he is still as popular as you can possibly imagine.

A Jewish Proverb

Question 45

You talked about different likes and dislikes and tendencies in different regions of the country. Do you see dissimilarities in different generations? Baby Boomers never liked hippies, and they don't like millennial either. Sociologists say that millennial and hippies have much more in common than yuppies. Does any explanation for this from handwriting analysis?

Answer

Your question is loaded and requires a great deal of explanation. However, it reminds me of a Yiddish proverb that says, "Why does Grandpa and Grandson get along so well? Because they have a common enemy."

When people get tired of doing the same things over and over, they introduce old values. Then they get tired of old values, they bring older values under the slogan of new values. Political incorrectness was the norm in the Sixties. The phrase 'politically correct' was perhaps first used in the late sixties. As far as handwriting is concerned, the introductions of personal computers have played a great role in millennial style of handwriting. Their handwriting may look different, but the results are the same.

Transforming Addition into Multiplication

Question 46

What is the secret of the president's financial success? Can you decode this from his signature?

□ Analysis

- Ability to see opportunity where others can't
- Ability to persuade people to work at their optimum capabilities

O Synthesis

The president's signature reveals that he possesses a great ability to see potential in a situation when most people will walk away. It also tells that he knows how to get the most out of human resources.

When an average man sees an acorn, he thinks it's something a squirrel can eat. However, when a businessman sees that same acorn, he thinks that if he sows it, he will grow a tree. When the president sees the acorn, he sees a forest.

Masculine Party and Feminine Party

Question 47

My question is about the affiliation of the party. Can you tell just by looking at handwriting whether a person belongs to the Republican or Democratic party or if he or she is an independent?

Answer

The short answer is no. The reason is that there is no such thing as a 100 percent Republican or Democratic. People join parties for different reasons. Ideologies play a role to some extent.

Let me share with you an interesting story. In the year 2000, when the Supreme Court announced its verdict in favor of President Bush about the Florida voting controversy, a friend of mine congratulated me about the verdict because I was a registered Republican and voted for W. Bush. I smiled and said there is a two-party system in this country. One party is masculine, and the other party is feminine. The masculine party won .He chuckled.

What I discovered in my research is that the Republican Party is more aggressive when it comes to compromising. Democrats meet more than halfway on most issues.

I-95 and I-40

Question 48

Have you ever conducted research that points out what people like or dislike and what their priorities in different states are?

☐ **Analysis**

- Product-oriented states
- People-oriented states

○ **Synthesis**

At one point, I was curious to know in what state most aggressive people live? And on one occasion a marketing manager asked me, "Can you give me some assessment about what state our product will have a chance to sell better in?"

I researched and gathered some data. The information provided the trend, but was not conclusive. The results were surprising. I discovered that the people who were most aggressive lived in the state of Ohio. During another research project, I discovered that the people who lived along I-95 from Vermont to Chesapeake were more interested in knowing more about new products than meeting new people.

However, people who lived along I-40 from the Carolinas to New Mexico were more fascinated by meeting new people rather than discovering new products.

Bi-Dimensional Approach

Question 49

Hi! I studied American History in my college years. I have been listening to the president's statement closely for quite some time. I noticed that the president sometimes makes statements without realizing the consequences of his words. What can be concluded from his signature making statement like this?

☐ Analysis

- Optic and visualization is dominant sense.
- What is not visible has a lesser value
- Instant gratification plays a greater role in the decision making process

O Synthesis

The President's signature indicates that his power of visualization is phenomenal; however, it gets jaded occasionally. He gets overwhelmed with optics and visual sights. He focuses more on the width and the length of the issue what I call bi-dimensional observation.

In his view the depth of the issue possesses a lesser value because it is not visible for an average person. He likes tangible results. Thinking about depth and consequences leads to uncertainties. It also hinders instant gratification, which is a big turnoff for the president.

A while back, I analyzed a few signatures of the harsh critics of the president just to find out the real reason behind the criticism.

What I discovered, most of this critics are tri-dimensional thinkers. i.e they focus more on the depth than the visible side of the issue.

Bernie Sanders

Question 50

I am assuming that you have analyzed Bernie Sanders's signature. What do you see in his signature that made him rise to the level of nearly taking the Democratic nomination?

☐ Analysis

- A philosophical bend of mind
- Means what he says
- Wants to see equality in every sense
- Highly empathetic and sympathetic

○ Synthesis

A serious thinking and philosophical bend of mind is manifested in Bernie Sanders's signature. He is a true humanitarian who believes in equality in every sense for everyone. He is empathetic as well as sympathetic at the same time, since he believes in equality at heart. He likes to see political, social, and economic equality.

What made him so popular was his message more than his personality. The message lifted up the messenger.

Being a serious thinker and observer, he perhaps realized that propaganda against socialism and egalitarianism had subsided after the fall of the Soviet Union. He saw the vacuum and the opportunity to spread his message. Since economic equality is a powerful message, millennials who had not been indoctrinated against it listened to his message with an open ear, heart, and mind. The message raised him to the near pinnacle of the Democratic party.

President Trump and President Obama

Question 51

I am pretty sure you have analyzed former president Obama's signature. What different approaches did both presidents use when it comes to solving issues?

☐ **Analysis**

- President Trump looks at the crust of an issue.
- President Obama focuses on the core of the issue.
- President Trump thinks in the present tense.
- President Obama thinks in the future tense.

○ **Synthesis**

Yes, I have analyzed President Obama's signature in depth. The answer to this question is so long that I could write a book just on analyzing all of his approaches and issues.

President Trump's signature tells us that he is very visual. He looks at the issues as they appear. He tries to find the solution by using sales techniques. He is always eager to see instantaneous results. He thinks mostly in the present tense. He feels every criticism is a passing shower, and no scandal is too big for him to handle.

President Obama's signature indicates that he looks at every issue from a philosophical standpoint. He focuses on the core of the issue. He looks at what philosophies are colliding and which philosophies are going parallel. He is extremely mindful of criticism and scandals. He thinks in the future tense. He wants to make sure his interpretation cannot be misconstrued.

Pardoning Himself

Question 52

The president has pardoned quite a few people and now there is talk about whether or not the president might pardon himself. Does his signature give a clue that he might pardon himself too?

☐ **Analysis**

- A belief that the perception of threat is more potent than the threat itself

○ **Synthesis**

The president's signature indicates that he believes that his style of description and interpretation make phenomenon much more powerful than what is normally perceived. He may justify pardoning himself as an available option. But he perhaps will never exercise this option. This option will stay on the table because it decorates the table well.

Short Term and Long Term Goals

Question 53

You have been analyzing the president's signature for quite a while. Have you figured out from his signature, what his short and long term goals are?

☐ **Analysis**

- Every promise is important
- Behind every promise there is mission
- Every mission must make history

○ **Synthesis**

The president made a long list of promises during the campaign. He wants to fulfill every single promise in a spectacular way. This is indicated in his signature.

What I have concluded so far is that he has both short term and long term goals. In the short term, he wants a landslide victory in the next election so the stigma of losing the popular vote in the previous election will go away and be buried forever. His long term goal is of course creating a legacy second to none. After the second term he might try to justify a third term. What I find in his signature is that he feels that traditions are in the mind of the beholder. People would agree to change the laws if they were educated properly.

Every goal is important to him, but I believe the supreme goal in his mind is to resolve the Arab-Israeli issue once and for all. Then he could be loved and worshipped around the world.

.

"Non-Prophet" Organization

Question: 54

The president motivated a great number of independents and people who never voted before to go to the polls. According to a recent survey, the fastest growing segment of voters is independents. Does the president's message influence people to remain uncommitted or independent?

☐ Analysis

- Likes multi-prong approach
- Likes to shake the status quo

○ Synthesis

I do not fully understand your question, but this is what I understood, that the president's signature shows that he likes to shake things up. He is influencing most voters' opinions. What he enjoys more is the feeling that he is shaking up people's ways of thinking. Uncommitted and independent voters are not necessarily the same. Hesitant voters remain uncommitted and take the position as independents. Independents are the amalgamation of numerous schools of thoughts, including the so-called uncommitted.

The fastest growing segments of independents are composed of secularists, agnostics, atheists, pagans, and other nonbelievers who don't like to be labeled. I call these people members of the "non-prophet" organization.

Relationships and Respect

Question 55

During the election campaign, some senior Republicans and lifelong friends supported the president with warmth and enthusiasm. These people were expecting that they would show up as part of his cabinet. Why were these key figures pushed aside? Does his signature show that he just wanted their support with no reward?

☐ Analysis

- Loves his friends dearly
- Real friends too close to him may cause discomfort

○ Synthesis

The president's signature indicates that he is extremely selective about his real friends. Once he accepts them, he loves them dearly. He doesn't want them in a situation where a clash of ideas could result in contention and the relationship could go sour. Sometimes he will feel it necessary to keep some distance from them. There is a rule in the corporate world that you never get too close to your subordinates because you never know when you have to let them go. One of the reason you don't see these people in the cabinet is because they were more than just supporters. They were kept out of the loop out of love and respect, and they should be proud of that.

Rule of the Rules

Question 56

The president said every two rules will be replaced with one rule. What benefit does he see in doing that according to his signature?

☐ **Analysis**

- Hates restrictions in any shape or form
- Enjoys rearranging what doesn't reflect his values
- Loves to leave fingerprints on anything he touches

○ **Synthesis**

According to the president's signature, less rules means less restriction, and less restriction means opening the wide doors for entrepreneurs. This is an age-old debate. The other side believes less rules open doors for bigger loopholes. The last financial depression was blamed on a lack of regulations. The previous Congress introduced quite a bit of restrictive laws. This seesaw game will continue as long as independents do not show their strength. Certainly, business people want less and less rules so their businesses can flourish easily.

True Republican and True Democrat

Question 57

You mentioned earlier that people join political parties for different reasons. They may not be true Republicans or true Democrats. Can you identify a true Republican or true Democrat from their handwriting?

☐ **Analysis**

- Thinking in terms of *we* or *me*

○ **Synthesis**

Yes, it is possible to identify whether a person is a true Democrat or a true Republican. What sets Democrats apart from Republicans is their way of thinking. True Democrats think in terms of *we*, while true Republicans think in terms of *me* a majority of the time. Republicans think in terms of *we* during times of crisis when they feel their interests are best served as part of the whole. Once the siren has quieted, Republicans go back to the world of *me*. You probably heard the saying, "We are all in this together." Most Republicans carry more vitamins "I" in their system than democrats. True

Democrats think in those terms in all types of situations. Democrats think in terms of *we* in times of crisis or peace most of the time. Based on this definition, it is not hard to identify who is a genuine Democrat or genuine Republican.

Utopianism

Question 58

You sounded like pretty big admirer of the president all along. I was shocked when you said you didn't vote for the president. What did you find in his signature that impacted your decision?

☐ **Analysis**

- Unwavering belief in utopianism

○ **Synthesis**

My decision not to vote for the president was not like disenchanted Republicans who voted against him. To me, those are mid-level differences. The foundation of those differences are based on indoctrination.

It is hard for me to explain and it is harder for people to comprehend my reasoning; let me try my best.

What I discovered in the president's signature is that he carries an unwavering belief in utopianism. My personal estimation is that he probably doesn't follow the full scope of utopianism. A utopian always sets their bar so high that an average person cannot even dream of. They are so involved in their mission that they underestimate the power of counter forces.

When a utopian crosses an invisible red line, which a majority of the time they are not aware of, a law of diminishing returns kicks in and turns assets into liabilities.

Utopians try to decorate and carve the jar so hard that sometimes they end up making a crack. Their general argument is, 'so far they have been winning, why not just continues their mission.'

Foreign Relations

Your feedback and comments will be appreciated at
ILYASZESHAN@gmail.com

Australian Handwriting

Question 59

I am from Australia. Can you tell just from looking at handwriting whether a person is from Australia?

Answer:

My answer may disappoint you. I would say no. There are some tell tale signs of what I call a touch of Australia, but scientifically and categorically, I cannot definitively say a sample of handwriting comes from an Australian. However, Australian handwriting is much different than typical American handwriting. In Australian handwriting, you can detect the influence of some Chinese values. Let me tell you how I describe an Australian. They look like Americans, talk like the British, and think like the Chinese.

Democracy in the Middle East

Question 60

I was on your website, and I found out that you are the inventor of handwriting analysis in Middle Eastern languages. My question is, why doesn't the Middle East embrace democracy? Why don't they see that equality is in everyone's best interest?

☐ Analysis

- Strong indoctrination against democracy
- A belief that honest and sincere people shy away from political participation
- Heads counted in Western democracy, not the brains

○ Synthesis

I have analyzed thousands of handwriting samples of Middle Eastern people. What I discovered is that they have been indoctrinated for more than a thousand years against Western democracy. They feel democracy is a fancy name for mobocracy where the crowd leads the leaders. The definition of right and wrong rests in the hands of the crowd. They wonder why people believe in democracy where heads are counted, not the brains.

ISIS and Terrorists

Question 61

Can you tell just by looking at the handwriting whether a person is associated with ISIS or a terrorist?

☐ Analysis

- Cultish mentality
- Excessive belief in supernatural
- Tendencies for violence

○ Synthesis

ISIS is a form of a cult. These types of cults have been around for hundreds of years in the Muslim world. The difference is that this cult has turned violent recently. Hundreds of these types of cults still exist, but they are unseen because they have not turned violent yet.

International Agreements

Question 62

President Trump is scrapping international treaties and agreements right and left. I just want to know why he is doing this. What does his signature say in that regard?

☐ Analysis

- Loves to reshuffle and organize things the way he sees fit
- Believes in handling situations on case-by-case basis
- Excessive interest in personalization

○ Synthesis

His signature gives a pretty clear explanation of why the president is walking away from those treaties. Signature analysis does not distinguish whether an agreement is international, national, or between two corporations. All it tells us is how the CEO will react when he or she sees old agreements. The president's signature indicates that he feels it's necessary to transform agreements in accordance to his values and priorities. One of his values is dealing with issues on a case-by-case basis rather than using a cookie-cutter approach.

“Dollar Trump”

Question 63

During the entire campaign, the president made the case against Mexicans and Muslims. I am surprised that he chose Saudi Arabia as his first foreign trip. What conclusion can be drawn from his signature in light of this?

☐ Analysis

- Excessive belief in almighty dollar
- Element of surprise always turns him on

○ Synthesis

The president’s signature indicates that he is highly judgmental just about anything. When dollars come into play, all considerations slip to the backburner. In the Middle East, the president is known as “Dollar Trump.”The president’s signature indicates that he has an overwhelming belief in the dollar.

His signature also indicates that he always shows an interest where he sees some sort of opportunity. His maiden trip to Saudi Arabia shows that he seems pretty eager to strengthen relationship with the Saudi’s. He must be trying to fry a gigantic fish.

Recognition of the City is Harder than the Recognition of the Country

Question 64

Recently, the president made a decision to move the US embassy to Jerusalem. The response at the United Nations was not received well at all. Why did moving the embassy face such harsh opposition? Didn't the president know what was coming?

☐ Analysis

- Burning desire to create a legacy
- Feel strained evaluating intangible variables
- Accepts only optimistic advice

○ Synthesis

Jerusalem is one of the most talked about issues around the world and least understood at the same time because of polarizing propaganda from both sides.

Let me be as brief and as objective as I can be. This entire assessment you are about to hear is based on my analysis of thousands of handwriting samples from hundreds of nationalities around the world over the last couple of decades. At one point I was very curious to know why Muslims felt East Jerusalem is beyond negotiation.

For the sake of objectivity, I will not use the name of the religions because such mention makes people emotional and subjective. Instead I will use ABC:

Religion A is three thousand years old. Religion B is two thousand years old, and Religion C is fifteen hundred years old. These three religions were born in the same neighborhood.

Religion A says that this city was their city three thousand years ago. Religion B makes no claim. Religion C says this city was theirs for 1,500 years until 1967.

Interestingly enough, residents of Religion B in the region sides with Religion C. Another interesting aspect of this phenomenon is that Religion C believes in Religion B and A with some differences, and you must believe in Religion A and B in order to be a true believer in Religion C. Religion C allows marrying only in religions A, B, and C. Other world religions are not recognized by Religion C. A great number of followers of Religion C are former followers of Religion A. Religion C believes that all three of us are the sons of Abraham, which means all three of us are cousins.

There is one very obvious characteristic about Religion C that's ignored by virtually everybody, and that is that they pray five times a day and pray for the liberation of Jerusalem, which is the ultimate commitment that's never found in any other religion in the world. Now Religion C population has grown so much that every fourth person in the world claims to be part of Religion C. In fifty-seven countries, they are a majority. In Russia, China, and India, they are a very strong political force. The intense commitment to their faith has been underestimated by experts.

A Saudi King once said that a sacrifice of a million Muslins for the liberation of Jerusalem would be a small price to pay. Muslims believe that their defeat in the 1967 war was their biggest defeat in their 1,500-year-old history.

President Nixon one time said that we should resolve the Palestinian issue now, or else it will be tougher as time goes by. The emotions are so high and commitment so deep that the demand for a one-state solution will grow, especially after the president's recent decision to move the US embassy.

Recognition of the city by Muslims is much harder than the recognition of the country itself. The president is trying to resolve the issue with materialistic means. This is a fight between materialism and spiritualism. Materialism always has a ceiling and spiritualism has no ceiling.

They Will Not Because They Cannot

Question 65

It seems that you know the Middle East quite well. In your estimation, was the president's decision in moving the embassy to Jerusalem prudent? Do you think the Middle Eastern countries will come into consensus eventually?

☐ Analysis

- A belief that reward and punishment can resolve any issue

○ Synthesis

The president's signature tells that he believes reward and punishment are the ultimate tools that can make people agree. The problem is that this matter is not in the hands of the Middle Eastern leaders. If any Muslim country moves its embassy to Jerusalem, that regime will be overthrown in days, not weeks. This is like asking a hundred-pound person to lift a thousand pounds. No matter what kind of reward or punishment is offered, they will not move the embassy because they just can't.

Trump and Putin
Who Loves Whom?

Question 66

Why does the president like Russian President Putin so much? Is it chemistry or something else? Can you draw any conclusion from their signatures?

Answer

I saw President Putin's signature a long time ago. I couldn't obtain it. I almost forgot the features of his signature. What I do recall is that he is a very complex politician. Contrary to popular belief, Putin is more interested in President Trump and not the other way around.

Putin feels that the breakup of the Soviet Union was the greatest tragedy of the twentieth century, and President Putin is the champion of the motto "Make Russia great again." An isolationist American president will create room for Russia to spread its wings comfortably around the world.

British Prime Minister Tony Blair

Question 67

I am from the United Kingdom. Have you analyzed the signature of British Prime Minister Teresa May or any other prime minister?

□ Analysis

- Extremely empathetic
- Extremely farsighted
- Extremely objective

O Synthesis

I have not analyzed Mrs. May's signature; however, I have analyzed the signatures of quite a few British prime ministers from the time of Mr. Wilson.

People used to ask me quite often about Tony Blair's signature during and after the Iraq War. His signature indicates that he is emotionally mature, farsighted, and objective. People used to ask me why he got involved in the Iraq War if he was that smart.

I have a theory about that, and in my estimation he was under enormous pressure from the United States. I believe he did something against his wishes. It was very hard for him to say no to the US president at that time. He didn't want to be ridiculed like the German and French leaders. Remember the "freedom fries" jokes about France in the United States? He was also under a moral obligation because the United States supported the UK in the Argentinean war and that was the time to pay off.

Thesis, Antithesis, and 2042

Question 68

You mentioned that you have analyzed Middle Eastern handwriting quite a lot. Why are their terrorists turning against the West? Is there any end insight?

Answer

The West began to feel threatened by the immigrants. The East has been feeling the pinch since colonization began.

Modern means of communication has shocked them even more. They see the everyday lifestyle of the West virtually live and that creates the feeling of alienation and deprivation among them.. The frustration is coming out in the form of terrorism. These terrorists are using religion to ignite the fire. It seems a cultural war is shaping up between the East and West. This phenomenon is shaping up as thesis and antithesis.

Whenever thesis and antithesis occurs, synthesis follows. As a matter of fact, this process of synthesis has already begun. Lots of Muslims and others are turned off with terrorism and leaning toward secularism and even atheism. It is predicted that by the year 2042, all combined religions will be in the minority and that atheism will be in the majority. In reality, Western religion is also an Eastern religion. Jesus was born in the Middle East.

Who Is Objective, and Who Is Not?

Question 69

I am from Vienna, Austria. I just attended the annual psychological seminar. There was quite a bit of conversation about right-brain and left-brain subjectivity and objectivity. Can you talk about objectivity and subjectivity from a handwriting analysis standpoint?

Answer

I cannot speak from a psychological standpoint. I can express only what I discovered during my handwriting analysis research .I have done some sampling, and I've discovered that Western Europeans lean more toward sympathy and subjectivity while Eastern Europeans tend to be more empathetic and objective (with the exception of Romania and some parts of Moldova which aligns more with Western Europeans).

As far as the left and right brain is concerned, you can reach someone who specializes in that field.

Afghan War

Question 70

The Afghan war is entering its 17th year and there seems to be no end insight. Now experts are saying that it is an unwinnable war. Have you ever analyzed the handwriting of Afghan people? If you did, what is your take?

☐ **Analysis**

- Afghan people believe more in spiritualism than materialism
- Afghan people believe that duty comes first, then safety
- Afghan kids start life from soldier to civilian, rather than civilian to soldier

○ **Synthesis**

Yes, I have analyzed large numbers of Afghan people's handwriting. As a matter of fact, I am the inventor of Handwriting Analysis in Arabic, Urdu, and Persian languages. My book was published on this subject not too long ago.

Afghan language is written in Persian script. Let me point out some of their traits that I discovered by analyzing their handwriting.

The value system of the Afghan people was not fully comprehended right from the beginning of the war. Afghan people are primarily 'Khatris' especially Pashtoon people. 'Khatri' is a Sanskrit word that means 'Soldier by birth.' This term was given by their enemies who had been defeated by them over and over. Interestingly enough, they don't like to be called Khatris. A 'Khatri' child would always want to be a soldier. If he was not recruited as a soldier, he starts life as a civilian. In other societies, a child grows up as a civilian and then becomes a soldier, if he chooses to do so. Their value system says 'Duty first safety later.' They do not have a concept of fatigue of war because this is their profession. War is a norm and peace time is vacation time. There are two types of Khatris - Muslim and Non-Muslim. Muslim Khatris believe in life after death. This life is finite and life after death is infinite. The motivation of Muslim Khatris is several-fold higher than Non-Muslim Khatris because of the belief in life after death.

Let me refresh your memory. During the Democratic National Convention a gentlemen by the name of Khan drew quite a bit of attention because his son received a purple heart and he was Muslim. The way young Khan sacrificed his life is a classic Khatri act, "Duty first, safety second.' Khan is a Muslim Pashtoon from Pakistan. A majority of Pashtoons live in Pakistan

Another reason why this war has gone on for so long is that its indirectly tied to Pakistan and India's relations. Unless the relationship between these two neighbors normalizes, the end of this war is not on the horizon.

China and North Korea Like 'Father and Son Relationship'

Question 71

The President and senior politicians keep insisting that China must use its leverage on North Korea in order to salvage the nuclear issue. I've heard that you analyzed lots of Chinese people's handwriting. Do you think China will help us to resolve this issue?

Answer

I have never seen the signatures or handwriting of Chinese and North Korean major players in this conflict, so I cannot be so specific about them. However, I have analyzed a great deal of Chinese people's handwriting and learned a few things about them and how they perceive the west and the United States.

First and foremost, the Chinese are more skeptical about the US than the US is about them. They call the United States a 'fair weather friend.' Once the issue is resolved, they say good bye and now 'you are on your own.' The Chinese call that attitude a part of the Bourgeoisie value system. Secondly, they do not believe in the theory 'talk,

talk, fight, fight,' being a friend on one side and an enemy on the other. I call Chinese people 'one track people.' Either you are friend or enemy, but you can't be both at the same time. They see the US is busy encircling China and at the same time expecting a friendly gesture on the issues vitally important to the US.

In addition, the relations between China and North Korea are deep seated. They feel they are a friend for good times as well as bad times. It will not be an exaggeration to say that this relationship is as deep as a 'father and son' relationship. The father will always be on the corner to protect his son.

China's leverage on North Korea is one thing. China can play North Korean card in its favor militarily and financially. On the other side, North Korea sees the United States as a big fisherman whose job is feeding, tricking and killing.

One Minute Encounter

Question 72

Prior to the meeting with the North Korean leader, the president said that in one minute he would know the outcome of the meeting. What does his signature say about his ability to make a statement like that?

Answer

For the president, every meeting is a sales meeting or sales presentation. When the president said that he would be able to gauge the situation and know the outcome of the meeting, he was not exaggerating.

In sales it is said that the first 7 seconds is the most crucial period of an entire sales presentation. A sales person usually knows in those 7 seconds whether or not his presentation will be well received with the gestures of the buyer or if the buyer is serious or mediocre.

Showing Video to North Korean Leader

Question 73

During the meeting with the North Korean leader, the president showed him a short movie. Some people called this un-presidential. The president sees the value of the movie, but most of us don't. Can you pull out the reason from his signature?

☐ Analysis

- A desire to communicate at gut level
- During the meeting he throws everything from his arsenal
- Always interested in applying some sort of sales technique

○ Synthesis

I mention occasionally the president always finds some sales technique that he uses during his meetings. Sharing the movie is one of prime example. This technique is frequently used in real estate sales, insurance sales, and especially in network marketing introductory sales. It is a practical tool since there were so many unknowns during the meeting, like language barriers, cultural barriers, and the risk of losing the substantive message during the translation. As they say, a picture is worth a thousand words and I would say a short movie is worth a million words.

The president treats other nationalities like Americans. His signature says that he assumes all nationalities' likes and dislikes are the same. In the western sales presentations, warmth and emotional appeal is the guiding principle. In eastern culture, cold facts are the deciding factor. The minute emotional appeal kicks in the eastern nationality antennae goes up and they expect the 'catch' is on the way.

From Peninsula to Pensacola

Question 74

Have you ever analyzed the signatures of the North Korean leader? If you did, what is your assessment?

Answer

I have never analyzed the North Korean leader's signature, nor North Korean people's handwriting. However, I have analyzed a great deal of South Korean handwriting. All I know is that North Koreans are different than South Koreans. My hypothesis is that they are much closer to rural South Koreans. North Koreans believe that they are real Koreans and South Koreans are contaminated by Western influence.

The North Korean nuclear issue is much wider and not limited to North Korea. Currently nine other countries possess nukes.

The sole purpose of possessing nukes is deterrence. North Koreans will never use nukes because that would be suicidal. North Koreans do not seem much concerned because they feel that they control two hostages – South Korea and Japan – both of whom live in glass houses.

Interestingly enough, after World War II, it was expected that Japan would try to take revenge against the United States.

There is a higher risk of accidental explosion or use of so called dirty bombs by any terrorists organizations.

If there ever was use of nuclear exchange that will contaminate the world environment, the effect will be felt from Peninsula to Pensacola.

Finally, if there were any large scale use of nuclear exchange, that will be the beginning of the end of nationalism as we know it. There will be a rise of humanitarianism and internationalism.

Criticizing Canadian Prime Minister Trudeau

Question 75

People were quite a bit surprised and dismayed when the president criticized the Canadian prime minister after the G-7 Summit. Why did he do something like that? There must be some kind of explanation in his signature?

☐ Analysis

- Extreme desire to surprise people in innovative way
- Showing anger at friends when in a good mood
- Gets furious at opponents when in a bad mood

O Synthesis

That was a classical act on the president's part. What I have discovered from his signature is that surprising people in an innovative way comes to him as second nature. Also I have discovered that he displays anger at his friends when he is in a good mood, which may be regarded a form of tough love. He gets really furious with his opponents when he is in a bad mood.

What I have extracted from his signature is that between the end of the G-7 Summit and the eve of the North Korean Summit was perhaps the most joyous moment of his presidency. His level of pride and confidence perhaps hit the sky. He honestly felt at that moment that he could manage the entire world single handedly.

Having said that, the disparagement of the Canadian prime minister was not directed to him even though it may have been perceived that way. As a matter of fact, it was part of preparation for the North Korean Summit. The subliminal message to North Korean leader was, "I can twist the arm of my friend if he is not fair and honest with me and I can break the arm of my enemy if he plays games with me. Get ready and be brutally honest with me.

USA Versus USE

Question 76

The President is renegotiating so many international treaties, including trade deals with the European Union. Europeans are getting uncomfortable with the initiatives taken by the president. Why does he think this step is important? Any reflection from his signature?

☐ Analysis

- Money is more important than relationships
- Achieving goal is more important than money
- Extreme desire to break records

○ Synthesis

The President's signature vividly indicates that once he set his mind to attain a specific goal, he puts the side effect of that action on the sideline. It seems that the goal is to bring more dough at home.

Your comment is quite correct that Europeans are getting uncomfortable with the new negotiations. Consequently several views are developing in Europe. A couple of them are worth mentioning.

The first view is that the president is a passing hurricane and the next president will be busy doing the mopping job. The second view which is more a matter of debate among intellectuals and that is if the President wins a second term, which is a high likelihood, this will be the birth of new US values. Consequently the cool breeze coming across the Atlantic so far will seize, which will make Europe humid. So the Europeans must start thinking about their own air conditioning system

Since the time of French President De Gaulle, Europeans begin to feel that U.S. is getting undue recognition. Europeans believe they are the center of civilization in culture and history. This type of feeling resulted in the birth of the European Union. They see the United State as the union of fifty states. In order to have a competitive edge they transformed themselves into the United States of Europe (USE) - known as the European Union.

Some isolationists, I call them "politically introverts," in the United States wonder why NATO was kept alive after the fall of the Soviet Union. The goal was to keep Europe in the United States column for an indefinite period. If Europe is lost, some experts believe everything is lost. The president is facing a dilemma between money and relationships.

Great Wall of America

Mind over Matter—If Mexico Doesn't Pay, It Doesn't Matter

Question 77

Why is the president so adamant about building a wall on the southern border? Does his signature shed any light on that?

☐ **Analysis**

- Anything big and huge turns him on
- Ability to obtain what he wants
- A yearning to create a lasting legacy

○ **Synthesis**

The president's signature clearly indicates that grand projects get him excited. Once his mind is set on a goal, he remains adamant about attaining that goal.

Perhaps he got this idea from the Great Wall of China. However, some people see this as the Berlin Wall, if it is built. There is a good chance a future Mexican president will ask a future American president, "Mr. President, tear down this wall."

However, the president has a point, and lot of people agree with him. Financing the wall is a contentious issue. I am surprised that the president has not made a case that the wall will pay itself. The wall would benefit by not only curbing illegal immigration but also dropping the border patrol budget significantly. This will make for great saving. Similar to a toll road, you make a one-time investment and then collect ongoing revenue. You will have residual savings every year once it is built.----So Mind over Matter, Sif Mexico Doesn't Pay, it Doesn't Matter.

Reciprocity

Question 78

I noticed that whenever foreign leaders visit the United States, the president talks about reciprocity. It sounds like it is one of his doctrines. Do you see anything in his signature that explains why this phrase is so important to him?

☐ Analysis

- Loves to give a new meaning to old terminology
- Expert in adornment
- Desire to create a strategy that goes over people's heads

○ Synthesis

Reciprocity is a complex phrase. The president's signature indicates that he possesses a great ability to simplify the message. It also indicates that he likes to create a strategy with a hidden meaning that an average person may not be able to detect. He has a great ability to define reciprocity in accordance to the expectation of the prospect and customize it as he sees fit.

Misinterpretation and miscomprehension of reciprocity causes voluminous divorces and break up partnerships around the world because everyone uses their own yardsticks. Some people believe there is no such thing as true reciprocity.

Man loves woman. Woman loves kids, and kids love hamsters. Reciprocity is nonexistent.

President W. Bush and President H. Bush

Question 79

My question is about the Iraq War. Why did President Bush decide to go to war with Iraq when the whole world opposed it? I am assuming you have analyzed President Bush's signature too.

☐ Analysis

- Overly optimistic
- Excessively passionate
- Extremely sensitive

O Synthesis

People used to ask this question frequently during the Bush administration. I wasn't too sure in the beginning. Then I started looking harder and harder to find the answer.

First, I discovered that President W. Bush is extremely passionate and extremely sensitive. He can easily get hurt emotionally, specifically in personal relationships. At the same time, he is extremely optimistic .I would say overly optimistic.

I developed a theory after analyzing the signatures of three presidents—President W. Bush,

President H. Bush, and President Reagan. Perhaps President W. Bush's role model was President Reagan and not his own father. In President Reagan's signature, I found that he always sounded more optimistic than he really felt. His charm could influence anyone. President Reagan was pretentiously optimistic. President H. Bush was cautiously optimistic, and President W. Bush was overly optimistic. Second, part of the theory states that there must be notable differences between father and son when it comes to the Iraq War, even though their differences never came out in public.

Judge Is Determined to Arrange the Marriage

Question 80

After analyzing so much about the president's signature, have you come to any conclusion about what is the number-one objective he want to achieve in this term or the next(if he gets one)?

□ Analysis

- Rarely gets sidetracked once his mind is made up
- Adamant on final decision
- A feeling of possessing a monopoly of wisdom

○ Synthesis

What I extracted from his signature is that he wants to create an immortal legacy. At the top of the list appears to be a resolution to the Arab-Israel conflict and peace in the Middle East hereafter. In this issue, both parties are further apart than they ever have been before. On top of this, Palestinians are no longer recognizing the United States as the arbitrator because of the recent steps the President has taken. It seems that there is a three-way standoff. Palestinians don't want to talk to their counterpart, and they don't want to talk to the United States either. The president is determined to bridge the gulf between the two parties and between himself and the Palestinians. He is adamant to arrange this marriage no matter what.

Love Dictators—Really?

Question 81

The president is widely perceived as someone who loves dictators. How much truth is there in this perception, according to his signature?

☐ **Analysis**

- Loves control
- Loves to expedite the process
- Proficiency extremely important to him

○ **Synthesis**

The president sees that dictators are in full control and remain on top of their situations. They do not need to beg for the support of their juniors. Juniors are supposed to follow the orders rather than create stumbling blocks by injecting their opinions. He sees that dictators expedite the process fast and proficiently. The private sector is a form of a dictatorship where it seems his values were cultivated.

Space Force

Question 82

The President recently announced the creation of 'Space Force.' It sounds interesting and futuristic. Is it possible to figure from his signature why he chose to create Space Force at this time?

☐ Analysis

- Loves creating history
- Enjoys memorable events
- Novel ideas turn him on

○ Synthesis

The president's signature indicates that his eye catches novel ideas quickly, no matter how much it is veiled. Creating a history is also a big turn on for him. This revelation certainly falls in that category. Space Force sounds like some sort of military force in space. As far as I know, there is an international treaty barring any country from weaponizing space. I wonder if this Space Force will have any teeth.

Fake News!

Question 83

The president often uses the phrase 'fake news.' What does he intend to accomplish by saying that? What does his signature say about that?

☐ **Analysis**

- Desire to verbally knock the opponent so hard that his head could spin
- No tolerance for talk back
- Desire to discipline anything that moves

○ **Synthesis**

The answer to your question is quite simple. The president's signature says that he has no tolerance for fault finders. This is his innovative way to rebut the objections.

Since the president started using it, the phrase 'fake news' has itself turned into news around the world. The joke is spreading like, "What is today's fake news?"

When people visit from overseas and see tabloids all over, they wonder why they are permitted to publish news like this. When they find out in tabloid circulation is greater than New York Times and the Wall Street Journal. They scratch their heads.

By the way, in a Southeast Asian country a legislature is working to pass a law for several year imprisonment for any media who promotes fake news.

Questions asked from 2015 to 2016

Your feedback and comments will be appreciated at
ILYASZESHAN@gmail.com

Messiah Complex

Question 84

Hi! I have never voted in the past. I am in my forties. I am very excited about Donald Trump's candidacy. Lately, people have started calling him a narcissist. Is he really a narcissist? Does it show in his signature?

☐ Analysis

- Having a feeling of being superior to anyone
- Excessive urge to be in the spotlight
- Uncontrollable urge to command
- Overwhelming feeling of that he can do no wrong

○ Synthesis

The Republican nominee's signature indicates that he has an excessive dose of *vitamin I* in the system. He feels no mother has given birth to a child better than him. He has an uncontrollable urge to command and control. He feels that he carries so much fire in his belly that he can lead the leaders. He might not utter the words but he feels that he is a king of kings. It bothers him when others don't see him the way he sees himself.

This kind of display of feelings is not welcome in a democratic society, but in some cultures the presence of this type of persona among them is a matter of great pride.

Psychologists call the person with this type of feeling a man with messiah complex.

Similar Personality Profile

Question 85

You mentioned earlier that the Republican nominee is a man with a messiah complex. Have you ever come across a similar signature that matches Mr. Trump's profile?

☐ Analysis

- Ultimate superiority complex

○ Synthesis

Seeing those with messiah complexes is certainly rare but not as uncommon as people might think. I come across people once in a while with this trait. Quite a few of them are in the sports industry, entertainment, and business.

I had a business associate who came one day on stage and confessed that he felt second only to Jesus Christ.

The messiah complex is much more common in Middle East and Central Asian countries than perhaps any other part of the world.

Political Correctness

Question 86

The Republican nominee makes politically incorrect statements frequently. I wonder why he makes statements like that. These statements are not helping him. Does his signature show the motivation behind that?

☐ Analysis

- Loves breaking old mold
- Gets more pleasure out of sarcasm than humor
- An urge to go against the flow

○ Synthesis

Going against the flow is an urge revealed in the Republican nominee's signature. Innovation is always on his mind. He loves deconstruct things and then reconstruct them as he sees fit. He is disenchanted with political correctness because it is boring and without action. The Republican nominee is a mover and shaker. He is always contemplating ways of breaking taboos, which is quite obvious in his signature.

Energy Level

Question 87

During the primary, the Republican nominee made fun of a few of his opponent's energy level. The Republican nominee sounds very energetic. I just wonder what his signature tells us about his energy level.

☐ Analysis

- Extremely high energy level
- Highly enduring stamina

O Synthesis

The Republican nominee's signature clearly indicates that he carries an abundance of energy and stamina. His energy level rivals that of most people half his age. The Republican nominee's energy level is genuine and real. He doesn't need energy booster drinks. Natural food can boost his energy level more than energy boosters.

Make America Great Again

Question 88

Republican Nominee has a slogan, "Make America Great Again." Why does he say that? America is already great. I don't get it. What does his signature say about this slogan?

☐ **Analysis**

- Ability to inspire people
- A belief in utopianism
- A belief in being second to none

○ **Synthesis**

The Republican nominee is a great motivational speaker who knows how to inspire people. This catchy slogan can percolate people's heart. His signature also indicates that he has a tendency to believe in utopianism. He believes that he can take the United States to the next level. The people who believe in utopianism feel that others do not know how to take full advantage of the opportunity.

He also believes that he can capitalize on his image. He believes that if he can bring pinochle financial success to himself, he can do the same to this country.

Power of the Poorly Educated People

Question 89

The Republican nominee made several shocking statements. I do not understand why he would say, "I love poorly educated people." Can you figure out from his signature why he would say something like that?

□ Analysis

- Ability to recognize who will get his message fast
- Ability to recognize where a soft spot exists
- Ability to recognize opportunity where most people pass

O Synthesis

The president's signature indicates that he recognizes quickly who will say hallelujah to his secular statements. He also has a great ability to identify who will embrace his ideas without counterarguments.

He recognizes a vote is a vote whether it comes from a college professor or high school dropout. A college professor will bring tons of objections and still remain uncommitted. A poorly educated person is an easy sale, and that person buys his ideas freely and without reservation when he or she sees a charismatic and flamboyant personality on the stage.

Naturalized Republican

Question 90

The Republican nominee's numerous statements in the past have resembled a Democrat's ideology. Is he a true Republican? What can you tell from his signature?

☐ Analysis

- Sees value on both sides of argument
- Doesn't like to be trapped in one ideology
- A craving to be uncustomary
- Results-oriented

○ Synthesis

The Republican nominee's signature indicates that he is free-spirited and wants to remain unconstrained at all times. Now he is standing on a Republican platform. According to his signature, this is his third priority. His first choice, which is his only dream, is to have his own party, preferably under his own name. His second choice is to run as an independent because he likes to be self-directing. His third choice is to be a Republican.

He sees some value in democratic ideology. However, his signature also shows that the Republican ideology, especially its economic outlook, makes more sense than Democratic tenets. He just wants to be part of win-win situations in any given circumstance. In reality, he is a naturalized Republican.

Mine Is Better than Ours

Question 91

I have been a Republican for all my life. However, I have never seen so much opposition for this Republican nominee from within the Republican Party. Can any conclusion be drawn from his signature?

☐ Analysis

- Loves to make provocative statements
- Loves to challenge both friends and foes
- Not a team player

○ Synthesis

The Republican nominee's signature indicates that he believes "mine is better than ours."This is the prime reason of controversy within the Republican Party. He likes to take a position that's different from others.

He believes in consensus as long as everyone has consensus around his proposals. He enjoys being a team leader rather than a team player. His signature indicates that once he takes a position on an issue, he remains adamant that his position is correct.

Rude Awakening

Question 92

During the entire campaign, the Republican nominee portrayed a gloomy forecast for America. The Democrats responded with the slogan "When they go low, we go high." What could possibly be the reason behind the pessimistic strategy of the Republican nominee?

☐ Analysis

- A belief in motivating through rude Awakening
- Master of drawing people's attention
- A belief that pinching works better than massaging

O Synthesis

This was not a pessimistic forecast. It was a rude awakening strategy. Interestingly enough, Democrats did not get it. They thought he was creating a "gloom and doom" scenario. His signature indicates that this was a very well-thought-out strategy. His signature also indicates a belief that pinching carries a longer-lasting impact than massaging. He tried to create a sense of urgency. The subliminal message was, "Get up and go to the polling booth. The house could be on fire!"

Love Gambling, Hate Casinos

Question 93

The Republican nominee used to own casinos. The logical conclusion is that he must be a gambler too. I am just curious to know whether his signature shows gambling tendencies.

□ Analysis

- Loves to take calculated risks
- Thrill to walk in uncharted territory
- Thinking about beating odds a big turn-on

○ Synthesis

The Republican nominee's signature indicates that he is an outstanding entrepreneur. All entrepreneurs take risks. They take risks when the odds are in their favor. Playing inside a casino and owning a casino are two different ball games.

The president can play inside of the casino for the sake of learning or entertainment, not to accumulate wealth. The odds of being successful in owning a casino are as good as any other business venture.

As a matter of fact, most casino owners look down upon casino players. They perceive them as naïve, and they capitalize on their immaturity. President sees casino as a business opportunity. Casino players see casino as a house of opportunity.

Neo-Antiestablishmentarianism

Question 94

Media and political pundits are calling the Republican nominee's victory a win against the establishment. Others are saying that when he is in the office, he will transform himself into one in favor of the establishment. What does his signature say?

☐ Analysis

- Likes to replace old wine in a new bottle
- An yen to rebel
- Mover and shaker

○ Synthesis

The Republican nominee's signature vividly indicates that he carries a burning desire to reshuffle and reorganize things around him. He is a mover and shaker. These urges are so deep-seated that it can be safely forecasted that he will continue to shake things until the last day of his presidency. The Republican nominee is a champion of Neo-Antiestablishmentarianism.

True Blue, Scarlet Red, and Purplicious

Question 95

The Republican nominee has changed his position on so many issues with the party. I wonder if he is really a Republican.

☐ **Analysis**

- Carry multiple opinions on the same issue
- Strong desire to stand alone
- Desires to create his own brand

○ **Synthesis**

The Republican nominee's signature indicates that he carries mixed feelings on just about everything, whether it is political or nonpolitical. The same is true with his ideologies. The Republican nominee is a true blue American. On economic issues he is scarlet red, and on social issues he is purplicious.

His signature also indicates that he sees good, bad, or even ugly in both parties. as a political convenience, he is standing on the Republican platform, but his heart says that he is at equidistance from both of the parties.

Trumpism
Non-ideological Pragmatism

Question 96

I am a student of philosophy. I am also a Republican. In the past, the Republican nominee expressed views that were much closer to Democrats. Is he a true Republican?

☐ Analysis

- Believe in pragmatism
- Lack of interest in complexity of philosophies

O Synthesis

Signature or handwriting cannot reveal which party a writer belongs to. The Republican nominee's signature indicates that he is only interested in instant results. This gives a clue that he is a pragmatist with no special influence of any ideology. Since he will embrace any idea that will provide results, we can conclude that he is a non-ideological pragmatist.

Tax Return

Question 97

The Republican nominee hasn't made his tax returns public. Do you think he will ever? People also say he is not as rich as he purports. What does his signature say?

☐ Analysis

- A shrewd planner in a specialized field
- Knows what to say and when to stay only on the subject he knows well
- Takes pride in his sales presentations

○ Synthesis

The president is a shrewd businessman, and shrewd businesspeople never discuss their source of income except with their accountants.

Figuring out how much an individual makes every year is beyond the scope of handwriting analysis. Handwriting can tell whether an individual is content with his income or not. The president's signature indicates that he is happy with his finances but not content.

It is not difficult to figure out how much a billionaire makes in the duration of a year. The arithmetic is simple. If a billionaire earns or enhances his wealth only 5 percent in a year and works forty hours a week, he is making well over one hundred thousand dollars an hour. See the formulation here.

50 weeks in a year at 40 hours a week = 2,000 hours a year
5 percent of a billion = $50 million in a year
$50 million ÷2000 =$100,000 an hour

Selling the Sizzle

Question 98

Can you pick out the most significant reason why the Republican nominee succeeded in securing the nomination from his signature?

☐ **Analysis**

- Originality in words and actions

○ **Synthesis**

This question has been asked frequently during and after the primaries. I am going to give you a short and simple answer. After analyzing the signatures of all seventeen candidates, I discovered that most of them have common denominators. All Republican candidates were selling the *steak*, and the Republican nominee was selling the *sizzle*.

My Affiliation with a Political Party

Question 99

Your characterization of the President's signature seems pretty accurate. With the exception of a few, my wife also agrees with most of your interpretations. My wife also wants to know your affiliation with a political party, if any, and why you have that affiliation?

Answer

I am glad to hear that you and your wife like my interpretations. As far as my affiliation with a political party is concerned, I am a registered Republican, but I have never voted for a Republican candidate after the 2000 presidential election of George W. Bush. I used to be center right, but now my leanings have shifted to center left. I believe that currently, this country is leaning center left. The world is leaning center left, and I feel much in harmony leaning center left.

My Handwriting

Question 100

My question is about your handwriting. Do you ever analyze your own handwriting?

Answer

Yes, I certainly do analyze my handwriting occasionally .It is free. I used to do that quite often; however, I don't do so as much now. When I am anxious or excited, I just double-check that my state of mind is reflected in my handwriting too.

Handwriting Analysis is a wide subject. Some handwriting experts specialize in questioned document examination, working with lawyers when people forge signatures. Some work with personnel departments in selecting the right candidate for the right jobs. Some work with law enforcement authorities. I specialize in Grapho-Therapy for self-improvement. In my consultations I show people how to get rid of negative habits and turn them into positive ones by making certain changes in their handwriting. Even simple things like how to cross T bar or placing a dot on top of "i" can make a mega difference. I have brought a great deal of change in myself by using established principles of Grapho-Therapy.

Pictorial Dictionary

Your feedback and comments will be appreciated at
ILYASZESHAN@gmail.com

A

Round at the top
Tolerance

Flat at the top
Mechanical ability

Stems crossed
Imprecision

Center stroke low
Low self-esteem

Stroke omitted
Inattentiveness

Knot
Organized

Slim stem
Inhibition

Starting with lower case instead of upper case
Obedience

Arc in the beginning
Avaricious

Circle at the end
Vanity

Circle at both ends
Ostentation

Initial stroke long
Decision made based upon previous experiences

Dot in the beginning
Sour memories

First stem long
Loves power

Embellished capital
Unconventional

Basin stroke
Superficiality

Downward stroke
Frustration

Compressed
Reluctance

Circular
Tolerant

Ending stroke absent
Bashful

Closed mouth
Concealment

Open Mouth
Verbosity

Hook in the beginning
Acquisitiveness

Terminal stroke short
Timidity

Triangular
Technical aptitude

Little inward loop
Self-deceit

Two inward small loops
Misleading nature

Long terminal stroke
Philanthropic

Terminal stroke weak
Lethargy

Terminal stroke blunt
Dogmatic

Beginning stroke sheltering
Pride

Pasty circle
Sensuality

Long initial stroke
Resentment

Terminal stroke upward
Unrealistic

Terminal stroke curls over
Safeguarding

Terminal stroke hooked
Persistence

Terminal stroke ascending
Adventurous

B

Lower arc broadened
Arrogance

Wide at base
Gullible

Narrow at base
Skepticism

Conical bottom
Perceptive

Outward twist
Self-love

Inward twist
Arrogance

Compressed
Inhibition

Roman letter
Practicality

Absence of loop
Elegance

Long initial stroke
Planner

Initial stroke circular
Humorous

Initial stroke hooked
Possessiveness

Reversed loop
Self-respect

Dash in the beginning
High spirited

Hook in the beginning
Tenacity

Retraced stem
Posh

Long tail at the end
Generosity

Print-like
Clarity of thoughts

Tall stem
Self-Pride

Excessive right bend
Susceptible

Ending with tiny circle
Greediness

Separated stem
Uncommunicative

C

Angular on the left
Vigilance

Outward hook
Opinionated

Semi-circle
Proficiency

Long tail
Egotism

Simplified capital
Good taste

Initial stroke extended
Dynamism

Initial stroke enrolled
Prudence

Initial stroke long
Detailed planner

Circle at top and bottom
Sensuality

Compressed
Caution

Square formation
Mechanical inclination

Conical top and bottom
Probing mind

Exceptionally large capital
Uncomforming

Stroke twisted inward
Tenacity

Terminal stroke weak
Yielding nature

Stroke coiled under
Indifference

Stroke upward
Impractical

Blunt ending
Strong convictions

Terminal stroke long
Reliability

Initial stroke hooked
Frugality

Initial stroke long
Hates imposition

Tiny circle at the beginning
Envy

Circular formation
Generosity

Vertical formation
Indifference

Backward slant
Poker-face

D

Stroke extended left
Dominance

Roman capital
Clarity of thoughts

Circle to the left
Pretentious

Embellished formation
Boastfulness

Inflated base
Naivety

Vertical stroke long
Immodesty

Left circle exaggerated
Ineptness

Vertical stroke unconnected
Incompatibility

Terminal stroke weak
Lethargy

Hook in the beginning
Possessive

Pasty circle
Sensuality

Long initial stroke
Hates imposition

Vertical ending
Unrealistic

Narrow base
Skeptic

Stroke curled over
Guard from harm

Terminal stroke hooked
Persistence

Stem very tall
Philosophical

Arc instead of stem
Cultural interest

Terminal stroke blunt
Strong values

Base open
Unreliability

Stroke extended
Protectiveness

Stem retraced
Traditional

Delta D
Literary interest

Stem separated
Uncommunicative

Terminal stroke heavy
Firm opinion

Loop at the end
Artistic

Hook at terminal
Persistence

Terminal stroke rolled over
Protectiveness

Terminal stroke weak
Submissiveness

Terminal stroke heavy
Strong convictions

Stroke descended vertically
Dogmatic

Terminal stroke twisted under
Indifference

Terminal stroke absent
Secretive

Terminal stroke near horizontal
Skeptical

Stem dwarfed
Loves freedom

Flourish at the end
Showing off

E

Conical at the left
Quick thinking

Long Tail
Arrogance

Initial stroke long
Planning before execution

Terminal stroke blunt
Strong convictions

Initial stroke extended at the top
Dynamism

Initial stroke enrolled
Prudent

Inner circle at top and bottom
Romance

Simple formation
Maturity

Stroke coiled over
Insecurity

Compressed formation
Cautious

Embellished capital
Unorthodox

Greek E
Interest in culture

Filled with ink
Sensuality

Stroke coiled under
Aloofness

Stroke twisted outward
Unyielding

Stroke ascended vertically
Speculative

Initial stroke with small circle
Envy

Conical top and bottom
Probing mind

Terminal stroke twisted over
Tenacity

Combination of two semi-circles
Perceptive

Circular formation
Generosity

Terminal stroke weak
Easy going

Terminal stroke long
Dependable

Backward slant
Unconcerned

Terminal stroke enrolled
Pretentious

Upward slant
Unresponsiveness

F

Top stroke extended
Dependable

Wavy horizontal strokes
Humorous

Hook on horizontal stroke
Greediness

Resembles figure 8
Alert mind

Precise cross
Ability to focus

Cross missing
Inattentive

Triangular bottom
Cynicism

Both loops balanced
Organizational Ability

Lower zone inflated
Physical dexterity

Upper loop tall
Creativity

Conical top and bottom
Quick-thinking

Visible knot
Managerial ability

Large, loose knot
Self-respect

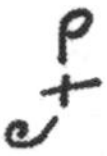

Multiple breaks
Poor health

Extremely inflated loop
Hypersensitivity

Terminal stroke with hook
Determination

Terminal stroke long
Flexibility

Terminal Stroke vertical
Unattainable goals

Terminal stroke weak
Intimidation

Terminal stroke heavy
Obstinate

Lower loop overblown
Erotic imagination

Terminal stroke curled
Pretentiousness

G

Flourishes in the beginning
Exaggeration

Upper part heavy
Perplex

Simple Formation
Good taste

Narrow formation
Conventional

Knot at terminal
Persistence

Arc at the bottom
Fear of responsibility

Triangular bottom
Decisive

Left slant with incomplete loop
Discomfort

Incomplete loop
Suppressed feelings

Lower loop overblown
Wild imagination

Lower loop extended to the left
Self centered

Both zones even
Pleasant attitude

Lower stroke long
Determination

Resembles figure 9
Likes figures

Resembles figure 8
Interest in social sciences

Lower zone exaggerated
Romance

Lower zone semi-circle
Hesitant

Reversed lower loop
Materialistic

Open-mouthed circle
Verbose

Narrow lower loop
Cliquish

Terminal stroke twisted down
Adamant

Lower zone open with enrolled end
Fear of unknown

Twisted downward
Boastfulness

Lower loop dwarfed
Low energy level

Terminal stroke vertical
Impractical ideas

Stroke coiled over
Insecurity

Terminal stroke blunt
Unalterable

Lower loop triangular
Decisiveness

H

Narrow and compressed
Cautious

Upper zone exaggerated
Spiritual exaltation

Upper loop extremely inflated
Hypersensitivity

Stroke missing at the end
Stinginess

Terminal stroke descended vertically
Domineering

Terminal stroke enrolled
Apprehensiveness

Long tail
Inflated ego

Needle-like point
Quick wit

Upper zone dwarfed
Lack of originality

Additional vertical stroke
Idiosyncrasy

Terminal stroke blunt
Strong convictions

Terminal Stroke with flourish
Show off

Terminal stroke vertical
Theoretical

Terminal stroke ascending
Bold

Terminal stroke short
Like obscurity

Terminal stroke curls over
Defensiveness

Terminal stroke twisted under
Inhospitable

Terminal stroke weak
Flexibility

Terminal stroke strong
Confidence

Terminal stroke descends vertically
Stubbornness

Hook at terminal
Persistency

Terminal stroke rolled
Generosity

I

Vertical stroke
Objectivity

Inflated lower loop
Self respect

Small in size
Lack of confidence

Terminal ascended
Deliberateness

Size medium
Modesty

Slanted toward right
Impulsive

Angular formation
Analytical ability

Slanted toward left
Introvert

Heavy dot
Passion

Light dot
Sluggish

Dot close to the stem
Detail oriented

Dot with heavy pen pressure
Certainty

Dot at right side of the stem
Quick-thinking

Dot as a jerk
Irritability

Tiny circle in the beginning
Envious

Dot like stroke
Enigmatic

Dot at left side of the stem
Procrastination

Dot like arc
Observer

Tiny circle
Pretentious

Dot missing
Absent mindedness

Hook at the terminal
Tenacity

Stroke ascended vertically
Impractical ideas

Dot right at the stem
Precision

Very high dot
Extremely Ambitious

J

Top heavier than lower loop
Ineptness

Flourished formation
Exaggeration

Simple formation
Good taste

Hook at the end
Strong willed

Arc at the lower loop
Immaturity

Triangle stroke
Resentment

Conical bottom
Observer

Stroke curled
Overly ambitious

Lower loop overblown
Daydreaming

Lower zone short
Lack of agility

Half loop
Confusion

Left slant half loop
Low energy

Loop extended to the left
Self-centeredness

Dot resembled an arc
Observation

Lower loop narrow
Selective

Enrolled ending
Anxiety

Dot missing
Inattentiveness

Ending stroke twists downward
Self-pride

Reversed loop with knot
Organizational ability

Stroke coiled over
Insecurity

Tiny circle in the beginning
Grudge

Stroke ascended vertically
Idealistic

Ending with heavy pressure
Surety

Dot with medium pressure
Precision

Dot at the left side of the stem
Procrastination

Light dot
Lack of agility

Dot very high
Self-starter

Heavy dot
Passion

Tiny circle not dot
Pretentious

Dot close to the stem
Good at details

Dot at the right side of the stem
Quick thinking

Dot resembles a stroke
Secretive

Small circle in lower loop
Clannishness

K

Second stroke long
High aspirations

Vertical stroke tall
Egotistical

Downward stroke long
Determination

Long tail
Arrogant

Knot in the middle
Managerial ability

Simple formation
Maturity

Small circle at the beginning
Enviousness

Backward slant
Withdrawn

Loop at the top
Argumentative

Reverse loop
Vanity

Terminal stroke descended vertically
Excessive love and hate

Hooked in the beginning
Hopefulness

Large circle at the beginning
Trustworthiness

Terminal stroke short
Stinginess

Terminal stroke ascended vertically
Unrealistic plans

Terminal curled over
Hesitate

Terminal stroke strong
Certainty

Terminal stroke ascended
Boldness

Terminal stroke weak
Yielding nature

Hook at terminal
Persistent

Terminal stroke with long straight line
Skepticism

L

Simple formation
Refined taste

Block Letter
Simplicity

Initial stroke enrolled
Prudent

Terminal stroke enrolled
Ostentation

Absence of loop
Urbanity

Initial stroke long
Planner

Reverse hook in the beginning
Opinionated

Hook at the beginning
Acquisitive

Reverse loop
Self-respect

Dash in the beginning
Optimism

Retraced stem
Cleverness

Initial stroke circular
Humor

Plain formation
Clarity of thought

Tall stem
Philosophical thinking

Extremely inflated loop
Easily hurt

Conical at the top
Sarcasm

Long tail at the end
Benefactor

Conical top and bottom
Sarcasm

Exaggerated bend to the right
Dependency

Separated stem
Uncommunicative

M

First arcade tall
Uncompromising

Compressed arcades
Introvert

Middle arcade tall
High goals

Large circle at the beginning
Responsibility

Initial stroke embellished
Humor

Embellished arc in the beginning
Dramatization

Initial stroke with hook
Rigidity

Tiny circle in thc beginning
Insecurity

First arcade tall
Mover and shaker

Middle arcade short
Agreeable

Terminal stroke crossed backward
Grumpiness

Capital resembled lower case formation
Humble

Arcade gradually descended
Leadership

Flat at the top
Mechanical skills

Resembled musical note
Musical interests

Circle at the end
Greediness

Initial and terminal strokes enrolled
Idiosyncrasy

Strokes enrolled
Immaturity

Rounded at the top
Creative

Threaded instead of arcade
Hasty decisions

Rounded at the bottom
Adaptability

Angular at the top
Analytical

Mixed slants
Confusion

Even arcade
Agreeable

Hook in the beginning
Unrelenting

Arcade with loops
Egotistic

Broken arcades
Maladjustment

Terminal stroke rolled
Charitable

Terminal stroke ascended vertically
Unrealistic plans

Terminal stroke long
Kindness

Terminal stroke with flourish
Pretentious

Stroke rolled over
Worrisome

Terminal stroke strong
Certainty

Stroke descended vertically
Excess in love and Hate

Hook at the end
Strong values

Terminal stroke descended
Pessimism

Terminal stroke ascending
Amicable

Terminal stroke with long line
Skeptic

Terminal stroke short
Secretive

Stroke twisted under
Indifference

N

Mixed slant
Emotionally unstable

Resembles musical note
Interest in music

Crossed backward
Self-destructiveness

Compressed formation
Shyness

Circle at terminal
Thriftiness

Even arcade
Friendliness

First arcade tall
Adamant

Flat at the top
Mechanical skills

Strokes enrolled
Impropriety

Tiny circle in the beginning
Resentment

Embellished arc
Hyperbolize

Stroke extended straight
Uptight

Initial stroke extended
Artistic

Terminal stroke extended
Hasty

Angular at bottom
Hard to convince

Threaded formation
Quick conclusions

Arcade with loop
Egotistic

Broken arcades
Nervousness

Terminal stroke weak
Idleness

Stroke descended to the right
Depression

Terminal stroke curled over
Defensiveness

Terminal stroke with inward hook
Persistence

O

Simple formation
Frankness

Formation resembled zero
Good at figures

Conical bottom
Quick thinking

Open at bottom
Insincerity

Long initial stroke
Hates imposition

Compressed
Cautiousness

Closed mouth
Secretive

Open mouth
Verbosity

Little loop
Self-deceit

Two small circles
Misleading nature

Hook in the beginning
Collector

Formation resembled square
Mechanical skills

P

Simple formation
Simplicity

Top stroke enrolled upward
Adventurous

Top stroke enrolled left
Artistic

Loop at both ends
Ambitious

Loop at the left side of the stem
Physical dexterity

Hook in the beginning
Possessiveness

Both loops balanced
Courtesy

Reverse stroke
Aggressiveness

Q

Downward stroke heavier than circle
Intensity

Lower zone heavy
Determination

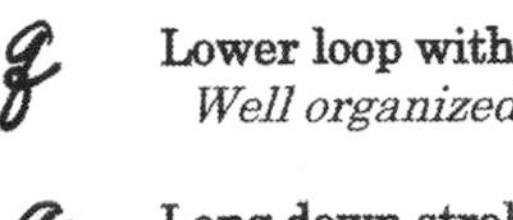

Lower loop with knot
Well organized

Long down stroke
High energy

Short down stroke
Low energy

Lower loop inflated
Sensuality

R

Simple formation
Good taste

Down stroke short
Lack of determination

Down stroke long
Determination

Vertical stroke long
Self-admiration

Break in strokes
Inharmonious

Long tail
High self-esteem

Small circle in the beginning
Enviousness

Large circle in the beginning
Enjoys Responsibility

Dash at the beginning
Cheerfulness

Two tiny loops visible
Egotism

Leaning Backward
Depression

Carefully stroked
Refinement

Rounded top
Versatility

Formation of two arcs
Urbane

Ending stroke short
Keeps low profile

Ending stroke long
Charitable

Ascended vertically
Pipe dreams

Stroke rolled over
Seeking safety

Stroke ascended to the right
Audaciousness

Stroke with flourish
Show off

Weak terminal stroke
Meekness

Descending stroke long
Single mindedness

Terminal stroke with hook
Unyielding

Stroke with straight line
Skeptic

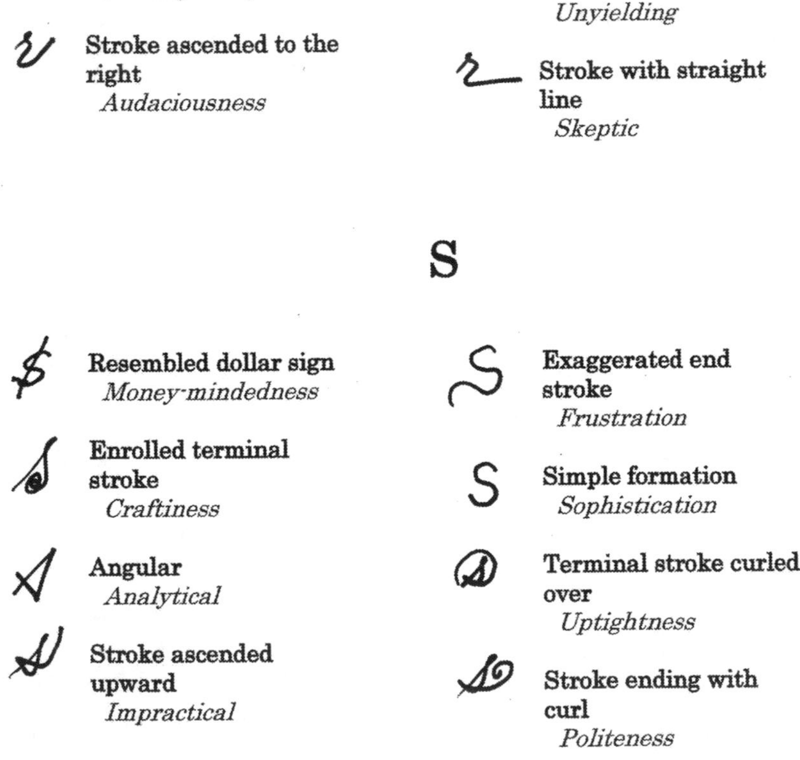

S

Resembled dollar sign
Money-mindedness

Enrolled terminal stroke
Craftiness

Angular
Analytical

Stroke ascended upward
Impractical

Exaggerated end stroke
Frustration

Simple formation
Sophistication

Terminal stroke curled over
Uptightness

Stroke ending with curl
Politeness

Terminal stroke twisted under
Dogmatism

Stroke descended vertically
Diehard

Stroke ascended to the right
Courage

Hook at terminal
Strong willed

T

Horizontal stroke long
Cautious

Horizontal stroke wavy
Humorous

Heavy bar
Strong sense of purpose

Horizontal stroke with hook
Eager

Precise cross
Accuracy

Bar weaker than stem
Lack of willpower

Hook in the bar
Collector

Tiny circle in the bar
Possessiveness

Long bar
Enthusiasm

Bar descending
Fussy

Horizontal and vertical stroke precise
Clarity of thoughts

Bar descending
Domineering

Concave bar
Passionate

Conical bar
Sarcasm

Ascending bar
Hopefulness

Convex bar
Superficiality

Small bar
Cold

Stem retraced
Formal

Bar above the stem
Extremely high goals

Separated stem
Low energy

Low bar
Low self-esteem

Short stem
Independent thinking

Bar forward swing
Takes initiative

Knotted bar
Managerial ability

Heavy at the end
Persuasiveness

Wavy bar
Cheerfulness

Resembled a star
Critical

Spread stem
Hypersensitivity

Bar to the left
Procrastination

Bar missing
Absent mindedness

Terminal stroke forms bar
Self-centered

Hooked on both ends
Unrelenting

Bar touching the top
Challenging goals

U

Needle-like points
Probing mind

Break at bottom
Insincerity

Backward slant
Unresponsiveness

Hook in the beginning
Cheerfulness

Small circle in the beginning
Envy

Large circle in the beginning
Enjoys responsibility

Simplified
Pragmatism

First stroke tall
Ego

Terminal stroke hooked
Resolute

Terminal stroke long
Cynic

Loops in stems
Impressionable

Vertically descended terminal stroke
Enthusiasm

Stroke ascended to right
Courage

Stroke with flourish
Melodrama

Weak terminal stroke
Weak will

Stroke rolled over
Safeguard

Long initial stroke
Rage

Hook in the beginning
Avarious

V

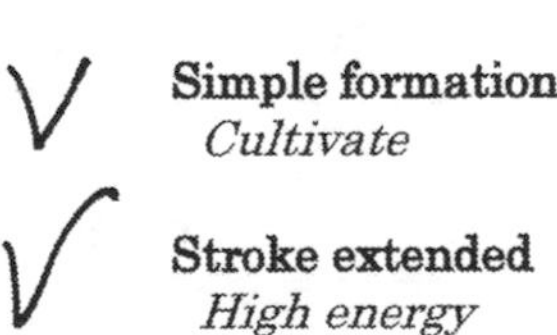

Simple formation
Cultivate

Stroke extended
High energy

Large circle in the beginning
Responsibility

Reverse curve
Facetiousness

Stroke crossed backward
Self-destructiveness

Angular bottom
Systematic

Hook at the terminal
Unforgiving

Light Pressure
Susceptibility

W

Terminal stroke tall
Day dreaming

Reverse curve
Funny

Simple formation
Down to earth

Stroke curled under
Self-centeredness

Terminal stroke hooked
Resentful

Angular bottom
Scientific mind

Wavy look
Lack of purpose

Terminal stroke long
Extravagance

Vertically ascended stroke
Unfeasible plans

Stroke curled over
Very careful

Large, circular stroke in beginning
Reliable

Terminal stroke weak
Wimpiness

Terminal stroke strong
Aggressiveness

X

Precise crossed stroke
Accuracy

Space between strokes
Talkative

Extended stroke
Stubbornness

Reversed loop
Remorse

Narrow cross
Caution

Embellished formation
Dramatization

Y

An arc instead of loop
Hates responsibility

Lower zone dwarfed
Indecisiveness

Incomplete loop
Immaturity

Beginning with flourishes
Exaggeration

Lower loop embellished
Overly imaginative

Large circle in the beginning
Decision-maker

Lower loop extended to the left
Self-centeredness

Plain formation
Refinement

Lower loop narrow
Choosiness

Small circle in the lower loop
Clannish

Lower loop triangular
Firm views

Lower loop enrolled
Fear of unknown

Lower loop resembles semicircle
Agree

Both zones balanced
Pleasant nature

Lower zone no loop
Prefers solitude

Stroke twisted downward
Self-centered

Lower stroke long
Strong determination

Slanted to the left
Unresponsiveness

Z

Upper part heavy
Incompetent

Simple formation
Practicality

Narrow formation
Introspection

Lower loop triangular
Resolute

Twisted ending
Egotistic

Lower zone exaggerated
Overly imaginative

Terminal stroke ascended vertically
Unrealistic goals

Both zones balanced
Pleasant nature

Lower zone with no loop
Instability

An arc at the end
Fear of responsibility

Incomplete loop
Latent imagination

Enrolled ending
Unnecessary fears

Lower zone resembled semi-circle
Quick thinking

Lower loop extended to the left
Irritability

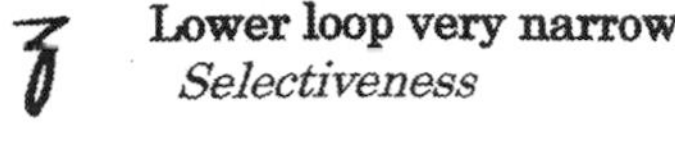

Lower loop very narrow
Selectiveness

Small circle at the end
Cliquish

Flourishes in the initial stroke
Theatric

Stroke curled over
Uptightness

Your feedback and comments will be appreciated at
ILYASZESHAN@Gmail.com

Printed in the United States
By Bookmasters